JILLIAN GLENN

Author of *Easy Low-Cal Vegan Eats* &
Light & Easy Vegan Baking

HEALTHY VEGAN
BREAKFASTS
& LUNCHES

· ·

60 Delicious Low-Calorie
Plant-Based Meals to
Power You Through the Day

PAGE STREET
PUBLISHING CO.

First published in 2023 by

Page Street Publishing Co.

27 Congress Street, Suite 1511

Salem, MA 01970

www.pagestreetpublishing.com

Distributed by Macmillan, sales in Canada by The Canadian Manda Group.

27 26 25 24 23   1 2 3 4 5

ISBN-13: 978-1-64567-673-7
ISBN-10: 1-64567-673-0

Library of Congress Control Number: 2022949677

Cover and book design by Laura Benton for Page Street Publishing Co.
Photography by Jillian Glenn
Cover image by Michael Vorndran

Printed and bound in the United States of America

TO MY FAMILY, FRIENDS AND READERS

When I went plant-based four years ago, I had no idea the adventure it would take me on. Three cookbooks and a lot of lessons later and I am still pinching myself.

My goal isn't to convince you to become vegan, it's to inspire you to enjoy more healthy plant-based meals so you feel your best. It's to provide recipes that are inclusive for all dietary needs. It's to encourage more balance in food choices. It's to help you create more beautiful memories with the ones you love.

From the bottom of my heart, thank you. Without you, and the grace of God, none of this would be possible.

Written with so much gratitude and love,

—Jill

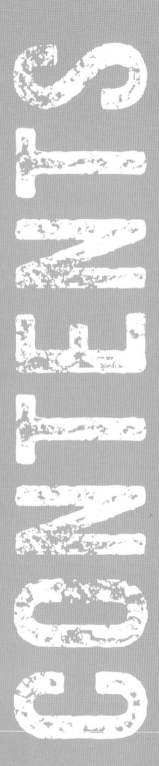

CONTENTS

INTRODUCTION

This is not your average breakfast and lunch cookbook.

What comes to your mind when you think of breakfast and lunch? For many people, it's hard to make these two meals healthy, interesting, and exciting on a daily basis. And we don't give their importance nearly enough credit.

Let's talk about breakfast. Many people skip it altogether because they can't find the time during their busy mornings or because they believe that skipping breakfast will result in weight loss. Unless recommended by a doctor, skipping breakfast is usually not a balanced long-term approach to health or weight management.

On to lunch. Many are perplexed by how to enjoy a healthy and satisfying lunch without totally derailing the day. So, we take the "I'll figure it out then" approach. Lunchtime comes, we're knee-deep in the day, and we're hungry. So, we either snack or we opt for convenience—oftentimes by picking up fast food or pre-packaged meals that are generally high in calories, low in nutrition and unbalanced.

I believe all meals are important, but when you think about it, breakfast and lunch may actually be the most important meals to plan for and to ensure are nourishing. They're consumed during the busiest times in our lives, meaning they should provide us with the fuel we need to get the bulk of our work done each day. Breakfast kicks off our metabolism and powers us up for meetings, caring for our families or our morning workouts. Lunch keeps us going through our afternoons and sustains us until dinner. Not only do we need to make eating breakfast and lunch a priority, but we need to make choices that aren't going to be calorie bombs, aren't going to spike our blood sugar and aren't going to leave us crashing later. Being healthy isn't just about eating a bunch of whole food–based meals (although this

book contains many of them)—it's also about balance and not restricting ourselves. That is why along with the creamy smoothies, nourishing soups, energizing salads and hearty lunch plates in this book, you will also find plant-based pancakes, blueberry muffins and even protein donuts!

This book is going to teach you how to build balance in your morning and midday meals. It will provide you with delicious breakfast and lunch ideas that are simple to make, use affordable ingredients, are lower in calories and high in nutrition! Whether you're looking for a quick make-ahead lunch to pack for the office, or you have 15 minutes to make something fresh at home between Zoom calls; whether you need a breakfast you can run out the door with or are searching for something to enjoy for Sunday brunch—this cookbook will have everything you need.

Every recipe in this book is designed to be a lighter version of breakfast and lunch classics, with a delicious, plant-based spin. Each one is under 400 calories to help you manage your health and weight without having to give up any of the foods you love.

To help you stay on track with your nutrition, I've included macronutrient breakdowns with each recipe. Many also contain nutrition tips in the introductions. All the recipes I've developed for you are designed to nourish your body (and some are designed to nourish the soul). Remember, while eating a wholesome diet is important for your health, it is equally as important to enjoy your food and enjoy life. Everyone in your home will love these meals, whether they are vegan, gluten free or a full-on omnivore! So, please enjoy with love and use my recipes to create beautiful memories.

BUILDING BALANCED MEALS

Food provides us with calories. Calories are energy for our bodies, and it's important to fuel up properly. Eating too many calories on a regular basis could eventually result in weight gain; eating too few, weight loss. The key is finding the right amount for your body. But calories aren't the only metric that matters. Eating high-quality, nutrient-dense foods in the proper macronutrient quantities are also main contributors for mental health, physical health and proper weight management.

Food is more than just fuel for the body. It can also be food for the soul. That's why it's important to enjoy what you eat. I like to follow the "80/20 rule," which means 80 percent of the time I eat food that's nutritious and healthy and 20 percent of the time I eat what my heart desires! For instance, my heart (and waistline) appreciate my flavorful weekday vegan bowls, my protein-packed salads, smoothies and oats. But my soul needs those weekend cinnamon rolls, fluffy pancakes and crisp plant-based pizzas! That 20 percent splurge is what motivates me to stay on track the other 80 percent of the time.

Let's talk about the foundation for building a nutritious and balanced meal. When I was going through my nutrition certification course, one of the very first things the instructor taught was the fundamentals of macronutrients. I found this information so helpful because no matter where I was or what ingredients I had on hand, I knew exactly how to build (or order) a balanced meal. I also learned how having all three macronutrients in a dish can help ease blood-sugar spikes, keeping us feeling fuller and more satiated—and curbing cravings later on.

As mentioned earlier, calories are units of energy our bodies use to do literally everything from growing hair to running a marathon. Calories are made up of the following three macronutrients:

PROTEINS: Often called the building blocks of our bodies, this macronutrient helps our muscles grow. I personally love protein because this nutrient helps us feel fuller.

Examples: nuts, seeds, black beans, chickpeas, tofu, tempeh, peas, protein powder (and if you're not vegan, eggs, meat, seafood and cheese fall under this category)

FATS: Fats get a bad rap for being high in calories, but a little fat goes a long way! Fat is a necessary nutrient and offers so many benefits from energy to hormone function. And I like having a little fat in each meal because it helps with satiety.

Examples: avocados, nut butters, vegan butter, coconut oil, extra virgin olive oil, flax seeds, chia seeds, plant cheeses, etc.

CARBOHYDRATES: Carbohydrates are our body and brain's top source of energy! And let's be honest, they just taste good.

Examples: rice, potatoes, flour, chips, tortillas, oats, quinoa, beans, fruits, vegetables, nondairy yogurt, granola, bread, pasta, popcorn

A lot of the foods listed in the examples above will show up throughout this book. And, with this foundation, you will now understand their purpose and the benefits they bring to your body. Whether you're making a meal using one of my recipes or not, look out for these foods to help you balance all your meals.

Another thing you'll see mentioned in this book is fiber. Fiber increases the feeling of fullness and aids in digestion. Fiber is found in many foods such as fruits, vegetables, legumes, brown rice, seeds, nuts and oats.

NOTES ON USING THIS BOOK

I have written this breakfast and lunch cookbook to be a simple and easy guide to making delicious and healthier plant-based meals for yourself and the ones you love. All of the recipes use affordable ingredients that you can find at almost any supermarket. Each recipe includes nutritional information and many include reasons why I believe the recipe is a better-for-you version. Here are some tips to guide you when interpreting the ingredients used, nutrition info, and other health information found in this book.

SUBSTITUTING PLANT MILKS: Many recipes within this book require plain, unsweetened almond milk, but feel free to substitute oat milk, rice milk, soy milk or any other plant milk. Nutritional content may vary depending on which plant milk you choose.

SWAPPING VEGAN BUTTER AND COCONUT OIL: Some recipes in this book call for vegan butter or coconut oil. These can be used interchangeably. However, if a recipe asks for butter, and you choose to use coconut oil, I do recommend adding a pinch of salt to the recipe to balance the sweetness from the coconut oil. If using vegan butter, calories and other macronutrients may vary depending on what brand of vegan butter you use.

OPTIONAL INGREDIENTS: You will find that some recipes include optional ingredients. Please note that nutrition information does not reflect optional ingredients, so add those to your final count if you are tracking your macronutrients.

STORING LEFTOVERS: Unless stated otherwise in the notes of each recipe, I recommend storing leftovers in the fridge for 3 to 5 days. You may freeze many of these recipes to extend the storage life.

RECIPE NUTRITION INFORMATION: Please note that all nutrition information listed on each recipe is estimated based on the ingredients used during recipe development. They may vary slightly depending on the brand of the ingredient. Any variations are negligible and the important thing is to stay within a healthy range of your desired macronutrients, not to obsess over hitting the exact number. For instance, the protein powder I use contains about 50 calories per two-tablespoon (30-ml) scoop and about 10 grams of protein. Yours may vary slightly, and this is totally okay.

MACROS AND CALORIES: Allow this book to be a guide for you to enjoy healthy, lower calorie, easy and plant-based meals that will nourish your body and taste delicious. Although nutrition information is important, it is not the only thing that matters. Every body is different and calorie and macronutrient goals are simply a range of what your body may need based on your height, age and activity level. Some people will need more than their estimated daily requirement and some will need less. It is important to eat when your body sends you hunger signals—even if you've already eaten more than your recommended daily calories. Eating healthy is about way more than nutrition and numbers. It's also balance—mindfully and occasionally splurging on foods you love (i.e. cinnamon rolls), eating without restrictions, and falling in love with thriving on healthy meals.

EXPERTISE: I have a certification in health coaching and nutrition. I've also been a food blogger and wellness enthusiast for many years. Balanced nutrition and plant-based/plant-forward eating has helped transform my personal health. And, I've seen it help so many others. But, nothing stated in this book overrides the advice of a doctor, dietitian or health-care professional. Listen to your body and see what works for you.

And, without further ado, breakfast and lunch are served!

QUICK &
HEALTHY
BREAKFASTS

Oh, weekday mornings! The time when we must quickly get out of bed, and jump into our daily tasks, usually with no time to spare. Some of us are even getting others ready for the day in addition to ourselves. Because we must go-go-go, we often put breakfast on the back burner. But a healthy, balanced breakfast is going to set you up for success. Fueling your body with something filling and nutritious can help energize you while you tackle all that you have on your plate. This chapter is going to make doing that super easy!

From smoothies to oats, granola to toast, this chapter is going to be your go-to for quick, healthy and on-the-go breakfasts. Some favorites include a delightful Tropical Protein Smoothie Bowl (page 13), delicious 5-Minute Blueberry Superfood Oats (page 17), mouthwatering Maple Vanilla Cashew Granola (page 14) and even Sweet Potato Toasts (page 26). In this chapter you will find an array of delicious, simple, lower-calorie, plant-based meals that are so easy! All recipes are made with healthy ingredients and are designed to make you feel as amazing as these recipes taste.

TROPICAL PROTEIN SMOOTHIE BOWL

Go to paradise with this creamy and nutritious smoothie bowl that will keep you full all morning long! The key to a smoothie is to have the appropriate balance of healthy carbs, fats and protein. Without all three, it may taste delicious but it might leave you feeling hungry before lunchtime. A benefit of having a smoothie is being able to hide greens in them. Feel free to toss some spinach or kale into your blender to boost the nutrients. You won't even taste it. This low-calorie smoothie bowl will take you 5 minutes to make, tastes like an island-inspired dessert and will leave you feeling refreshed.

Carefully cut the frozen banana into slices and add to a blender. Add the coconut milk, almond milk, protein powder, mango and spinach (if using) to the blender. You may also add a few cubes of ice to make the smoothie thicker. Blend until smooth and creamy, then pour the smoothie into a bowl.

Before serving, top the smoothie bowl with your choice of kiwi slices, mango slices, strawberries, shredded coconut, additional bananas, granola or pumpkin seeds. Pumpkin seeds are very tasty with this and add a nice crunch, extra nutrients, plus some more protein and healthy fat! Calories/macros vary depending on which toppings you use.

YIELD: 1 smoothie bowl

NUTRITION INFORMATION PER BOWL (NOT INCLUDING OPTIONAL TOPPINGS)
CALORIES: 303
FAT: 11 g
CARBS: 41 g
PROTEIN: 14 g

TROPICAL PROTEIN SMOOTHIE

1 medium overripe frozen banana

2 tbsp (30 ml) coconut milk

¾ cup (180 ml) plain unsweetened almond milk

1 scoop (2 tbsp [20 g]) vegan vanilla-flavored protein powder

½ cup (70 g) frozen mango

1 cup (30 g) spinach or kale, optional

4–6 ice cubes, optional

CHOOSE YOUR SMOOTHIE BOWL TOPPINGS

¼ cup (44 g) kiwi slices, adds about 25 calories

¼ cup (40 g) mango slices, adds about 25 calories

¼ cup (42 g) sliced strawberries, adds about 10 calories

2 tbsp (11 g) unsweetened shredded coconut, adds about 35 calories

¼ sliced banana, adds about 25 calories

2 tbsp (14 g) granola of choice, adds about 65 calories

2 tbsp (18 g) pumpkin seeds, substitute any nut or seed, adds about 75 calories

¼ cup (60 ml) maple syrup, plus more for drizzling

¼ cup (60 ml) melted coconut oil or vegan butter

2 tsp (10 ml) vanilla extract

1 tsp cinnamon

1½ cups (42 g) rice cereal

2 cups (180 g) rolled oats, gluten-free if needed

⅔ cup (97 g) cashew halves

¼ cup (34 g) sunflower seeds

½ cup (60 g) whole or chopped walnuts

¼ cup (36 g) dried fruit, optional; I use raisins

Sea salt

MAPLE VANILLA CASHEW GRANOLA

Skip that store-bought granola and make it yourself in the comfort of your own home. But, I must warn you: This stuff is addictive! The good news is that unlike most store-bought granolas, this is preservative free, has minimal added sugar, is low in calories and is loaded with healthful and wholesome ingredients. Oh, and it's completely free of any animal products or gluten! This granola tastes and smells amazing! Serve this gluten-free goodness on its own as a snack, or topped over vegan yogurt or smoothies for a healthy plant-based addition to your breakfast.

Preheat the oven to 300°F (150°C). Line a baking sheet with parchment paper.

In a small bowl, mix the maple syrup, melted coconut oil, vanilla and cinnamon. Set aside.

In a large bowl, mix the rice cereal, rolled oats, cashews, sunflower seeds, walnuts and dried fruit. Drizzle the maple syrup mixture on top, mix until evenly coated, then spread the granola evenly over the parchment-lined baking sheet. If you would like, you may also add a drizzle of maple syrup on top for added sweetness (note that this will affect the macros). Sprinkle the mixture with sea salt.

Bake for 25 minutes. If you would like the granola to be more golden, after baking broil for 1 minute. Allow the granola to cool completely. Serve the granola on its own or on top of a yogurt bowl or smoothie.

To store the granola, transfer it to an airtight container and keep in a cool, dry place or refrigerate for 7 to 10 days.

5-MINUTE BLUEBERRY SUPERFOOD OATS

One of my favorite ways to start the day is with a warm bowl of oatmeal. A lot of people steer away from oats because they are a carb, but this grain is also rich in fiber, important vitamins and other nutrients that we need to feel our best. In fact, oats have been known to improve heart health, making them one of the healthiest breakfast carbs! This powerhouse bowl of oatmeal goodness is taken to the next level with the addition of superfoods like flax seeds, chia seeds and blueberries. They will keep you feeling fuller longer and they taste so much better than any store-bought oats you will find.

Add the water to a small or medium pot and bring to a boil over medium heat. Add the oats and cook for 5 to 7 minutes, stirring often, until the oats are creamy. Remove the oats from the heat and add the frozen blueberries, chia seeds, flaxseeds, vanilla and maple syrup (if using). Mix until the oats are blue and creamy.

Serve the oats in a bowl topped with the mixed berries, banana and your favorite nut butter. Serve warm!

HEALTHY TIPS: Make extra-creamy oats by using ½ cup (120 ml) of plain unsweetened almond or oat milk in place of ½ cup (120 ml) of the water when cooking. This adds about 15 calories.

To add sweetness to your oats, mix in maple syrup or use half of an overripe banana, mashed, mixed into the oats. This will add about 50 calories to your oatmeal bowl.

Level up your protein by adding a scoop (2 tbsp [20 g]) of vanilla plant-based protein powder to these oats, which will keep you fuller even longer! This adds about 50 calories, depending on the protein used.

YIELD: 1 bowl

NUTRITION INFORMATION PER BOWL
CALORIES: 396
FATS: 16 g
CARBS: 56 g
PROTEIN: 12 g

1½ cups (360 ml) water, see Healthy Tips

½ cup (45 g) old-fashioned rolled oats, gluten-free if needed

½ cup (70 g) frozen wild blueberries

½ tbsp (6 g) chia seeds

½ tbsp (3 g) ground flaxseeds

1 tsp vanilla extract

1 tbsp (15 ml) maple syrup, optional, see Healthy Tips

¼ cup (36 g) mixed berries, I used raspberries, blackberries, and a few more blueberries

¼ sliced ripe banana

1 tbsp (16 g) nut butter, I prefer almond butter or peanut butter

NUTRITION INFORMATION
PER SMOOTHIE
CALORIES: 303
FAT: 12 g
CARBS: 39 g
PROTEIN: 11 g

½ frozen overripe banana

1 tbsp (16 g) creamy peanut butter

2 tbsp (12 g) peanut butter powder

½ cup (70 g) frozen strawberries

½ cup (70 g) frozen blueberries

1 cup (67 g) kale

1 cup (240 ml) plain unsweetened almond milk

ENERGIZING PB&J SMOOTHIE

I couldn't write a healthy breakfast cookbook without including my favorite smoothie! Growing up, peanut butter and jelly sandwiches were my ultimate comfort food. As an adult, I still enjoy these flavors but in a healthier way! This PB&J smoothie uses berries instead of jelly, has no added sugar and uses a little frozen banana and peanut butter to make it super creamy. I love starting my mornings with it because the flavor combo is absolutely irresistible and it leaves me feeling super full. This plant-based smoothie is protein packed and is also a great way to sneak some extra greens into your day without even noticing that they are there!

Add the banana, peanut butter, peanut butter powder, strawberries, blueberries, kale and almond milk to a blender and blend until smooth. Enjoy immediately.

HEALTHY TIP: Did you know that including fat and protein (like peanut butter) in your smoothies make them more filling and satisfying? It also helps keep you fuller longer!

PEANUT BUTTER & JELLY OVERNIGHT OATS

They don't call me Peanut Butter and Jilly for nothing! It's hard to beat this flavor combo and it's even harder to beat a creamy jar of overnight oats awaiting you in the fridge. Overnight oats are a popular breakfast because they are so easy! And, you will love this recipe that's flavored with peanut butter and "jelly." We don't actually use any jelly in this recipe (to keep it healthier and with less added sugar) but you won't even miss it!

Add the oats to a jar. Add the almond milk, peanut butter, flaxseed meal and maple syrup (if using). Mix well, until the peanut butter is completely incorporated into the oats. Store in the sealed jar in the refrigerator overnight. When ready to serve, top with berries, bananas and drizzle with more peanut butter if desired.

YIELD: 1 bowl

NUTRITION INFORMATION PER BOWL
CALORIES: 346
FAT: 16 g
CARBS: 41 g
PROTEIN: 12 g

½ cup (45 g) oats, gluten-free if needed

1 cup (240 ml) plain unsweetened almond milk

1 tbsp (16 g) creamy peanut butter, plus more for drizzling if desired

1 tbsp (6 g) flaxseed meal or chia seeds

1 tbsp (15 ml) maple syrup, optional

¼ cup (36 g) mixed blueberries and strawberries

¼ cup (38 g) banana slices

NUTRITION INFORMATION
PER PARFAIT

CALORIES: 399

FAT: 14 g

CARBS: 67 g

PROTEIN: 6 g

5-MINUTE YOGURT PARFAIT

There's just something so refreshing about a yogurt parfait. It's almost like having a healthier ice cream for breakfast. And, it's so convenient when eating on the go or between meetings! Yogurt is a gut-friendly and protein-rich breakfast. When I first stopped eating dairy, nondairy yogurts weren't nearly as easy to find (or as delicious) as they are today. We've come a long way with plant-based alternatives and now, us dairy-free folks get to enjoy this wholesome breakfast with ease.

⅔ cup (160 ml) plain unsweetened nondairy yogurt

½ ripe banana, sliced

1 cup (144 g) mixed berries

⅓ cup (36 g) granola of any kind (or use my Maple Vanilla Cashew Granola on page 14; see Healthy Tip)

Add half of the nondairy yogurt to the bottom of a bowl or mason jar, then top with half of the banana slices, half of the berries and half of the granola. Repeat with another layer of the ingredients. Serve cool.

You can eat this yogurt parfait immediately or store it in the fridge overnight for a delicious healthy grab-and-go breakfast!

HEALTHY TIP: When choosing store-bought granola, try to find a type that has minimal sugar—less than 7 or 8 grams per serving is ideal—and includes nutrient-dense ingredients like nuts, seeds or dried fruit.

HIDDEN VEGGIE STRAWBERRY BANANA SMOOTHIE

This creamy smoothie tastes like a dessert but is deceptively good for you. It's a complete and balanced meal thanks to the healthy fats and protein from the nuts and seeds. If you have any picky eaters in your household and are looking for a way to incorporate some healthy fruits, veggies and seeds, give this recipe a try! No one will notice the hidden veggies!

Blend the strawberries, banana, cauliflower rice, almond milk, chia seeds, date and almond butter until creamy. Serve immediately or store in the fridge for up to 24 hours.

YIELD: 1 smoothie

NUTRITION INFORMATION PER SMOOTHIE
CALORIES: 316
FAT: 15 g
CARBS: 43 g
PROTEIN: 10 g

1 cup (144 g) strawberries

½ frozen ripe banana

1 cup (115 g) frozen cauliflower rice

1 cup (240 ml) plain unsweetened almond milk

1 tbsp (12 g) chia seeds

1 date

1 tbsp (16 g) almond butter

YIELD: 4 (2-slice) servings

NUTRITION INFORMATION PER SERVING

EVERYTHING AVOCADO

CALORIES: 360

FAT: 28 g

CARBS: 24 g

PROTEIN: 6 g

BURRITO

CALORIES: 320

FAT: 20 g

CARBS: 31 g

PROTEIN: 7 g

PEANUT BUTTER BANANA

CALORIES: 266

FAT: 16 g

CARBS: 24 g

PROTEIN: 10 g

ALMOND BUTTER & APPLE CINNAMON

CALORIES: 306

FAT: 18 g

CARBS: 33 g

PROTEIN: 8 g

BERRIES & CREAM

CALORIES: 231

FATS: 14 g

CARBS: 21 g

PROTEIN: 5 g

SWEET POTATO TOASTS FIVE WAYS

Let's level up that basic slice of bread with a healthier superfood twist! Sweet potato slices are a tasty, fun and gluten-free alternative to sliced bread. They're also fiber-filled and way more nutrient dense than bread. Serve it your way by adding vegan cream cheese and berries, almond butter and apples, peanut butter and banana, avocado and everything bagel seasoning or any other ideas you can think of!

SWEET POTATO TOASTS

2 sweet potatoes

Olive oil, avocado oil or coconut oil spray

EVERYTHING AVOCADO STYLE

½ avocado, sliced

2 tbsp (24 g) Everything but the Bagel Seasoning

BURRITO STYLE

½ avocado, sliced

½ cup (86 g) black beans

2 tbsp (30 ml) pico de gallo

PEANUT BUTTER BANANA STYLE

2 tbsp (32 g) peanut butter

½ banana, sliced

ALMOND BUTTER & APPLE CINNAMON STYLE

2 tbsp (32 g) almond butter

4–6 apple slices

Cinnamon, for sprinkling

BERRIES & CREAM STYLE

4 tbsp (58 g) vegan cream cheese

½ cup (72 g) berries of your choice

Preheat an oven or toaster oven to 375°F (190°C). Line a baking sheet with parchment paper or foil.

Slice the sweet potatoes into ¼-inch (6-mm) slices (four to five slices per sweet potato). Spray the slices with olive oil, avocado oil or coconut oil spray and bake for 5 minutes. Flip, then bake for another 5 minutes, or until tender.

Divide the topping of your choice between 2 slices of sweet potato and enjoy!

NOTE: Two medium-sized sweet potatoes will make about 8 slices of toast. Each serving is about 2 slices. But, remember to eat until you are full and satisfied! Store leftover sweet potatoes (without toppings) in the fridge for about 3 days. Reheat by crisping them up again in a toaster oven.

APPLE CINNAMON PROTEIN OATS

Growing up, one of my favorite quick and healthy-ish breakfasts was a packet of instant apple cinnamon oatmeal. I say healthy-ish because while my heart was in the right place, and oats are definitely a great source of fiber and healthy carbs, those little packets were packed with sugar. And, while they may have been lower in calories, they didn't contain any additional fat or protein to balance them. Hello blood sugar spike! Here is a healthier and more balanced version of that nostalgic breakfast that tastes even better. You can even prepare it ahead if you'd like (see Note)!

To make the apples, heat a skillet over medium heat. Add the vegan butter. When the butter is melted, add the apple and cinnamon. Cook, stirring, for about 5 minutes, until the apple is tender. Remove the pan from the heat and set aside.

To make the oats, bring a small pot with the oats, water and milk to a boil over medium heat. When the oats begin to bubble and thicken, cook for another 1 minute, stirring. Remove from the heat and let them sit for 1 minute to thicken more. Then, add the protein powder, cinnamon and vanilla. Stir until creamy, adding a splash more almond or oat milk if it is too thick.

Pour the oats into a bowl and serve topped with the tender apples and nuts. You may also enjoy this with a nut butter. If you desire more sweetness, add the maple syrup and mix. You have control over the amount of sugar added! Enjoy warm.

NOTE: You can prepare the apples and oats in advance and store them separately in the fridge until ready to use. To reheat, place the oats with a splash of almond milk in a bowl and stir. Add the apples and heat in the microwave for 30 to 60 seconds, or until warm. I recommend only storing the cooked oats in the fridge for 1 day.

HEALTHY TIP: When shopping for plant-based protein powder, look for varieties that contain little to no added sugar, natural flavors, dyes or other additives. Also, you may want to watch out for mentions of "natural flavors" as many studies show "natural flavors" can actually contain preservatives and other unhealthy chemicals. I like using pea protein and try to find brands that include only two to three ingredients on the nutrition label.

YIELD: 1 bowl

NUTRITION INFORMATION PER BOWL
CALORIES: 400
FATS: 15 g
CARBS: 44 g
PROTEIN: 26 g

APPLES
½ tsp vegan butter or coconut oil

½ apple, diced

1 tsp cinnamon

PROTEIN OATS
½ cup (45 g) rolled oats or quick oats, gluten-free if needed

1 cup (240 ml) water

½ cup (120 ml) plain unsweetened almond or oat milk

1 scoop (2 tbsp [20 g]) vegan vanilla-flavored protein powder (see Healthy Tip)

½ tsp cinnamon

1 tsp vanilla extract

TOPPINGS
2 tbsp (14 g) pecans or walnuts, or any other nut, nutrition info may vary

1 tbsp (16 g) nut butter, optional, adds about 100 calories

1 tbsp (15 ml) maple syrup, optional, adds about 50 calories

PLANT-POWERED GREEN SMOOTHIE

It doesn't get any healthier than a green smoothie to start the day! Channel your inner goddess with this nutrient-dense powerhouse! This smoothie recipe is one of my go-to breakfasts for when I'm getting myself back on track after traveling or a fun weekend dining out. Did you know that ripe bananas contain less enzyme-resistant starch, making them easier to digest than unripe bananas? This green smoothie is filling enough to replace an entire meal because the banana, seeds, nuts and greens provide all the healthy fats, carbs and protein we aim for.

Add the banana, protein powder, almond milk, almond butter, spinach, almonds, flax seeds, chia seeds and a dash of cinnamon to a blender. Feel free to add a few cubes of ice to make it thicker. Blend until creamy. Taste test and add a half or one whole date to make your smoothie sweeter. Serve immediately, or store in the fridge for up to 24 hours.

YIELD: 1 smoothie

NUTRITION INFORMATION PER SMOOTHIE
CALORIES: 399
FAT: 9 g
CARBS: 31 g
PROTEIN: 6 g

1 overripe banana, sliced

1 scoop (2 tbsp [20 g]) vegan vanilla-flavored protein powder

1 cup (240 ml) plain unsweetened almond milk

1 tbsp (16 g) almond butter

1 cup (30 g) spinach or kale

1 tbsp (9 g) almonds

½ tbsp (5 g) flax seeds

½ tbsp (6 g) chia seeds

Cinnamon

Ice cubes, optional

1 date, optional for added sweetness, adds about 25 calories

GOODIES FROM THE GRIDDLE

I know what you're thinking, who has time to have pancakes and waffles on a busy weekday morning? Now, you do! That's because the recipes in this chapter will take you fewer than 20 minutes to make. And, most of them are freezer-friendly, meaning that you enjoy them fresh or store them in your freezer. Pull them out when you need a quick toaster or microwave-friendly breakfast treat. Thanks to this chapter, there are no excuses to skip breakfast or settle for something that's not delicious!

Within this chapter, you will find creative and filling pancake, waffle and toast recipes that are as easy as they are delicious! We focus on balance and sneaking in healthier ingredients to each recipe to keep your nutrition on track. From golden and crisp Chocolate Chip Protein Waffles (page 35) to 6-Ingredient Banana Bread French Toast (page 47), each recipe is vegan, gluten-free and waistline-friendly!

CHOCOLATE CHIP PROTEIN WAFFLES

Anyone else grow up loving frozen toaster waffles? My brother and I used to have them almost every weekday morning! For those who want to experience that golden, buttery, toaster-style waffle—while still watching your waistline—this recipe is for you! You only need 6 simple ingredients and about 20 minutes to make them. These waffles are under 80 calories a pop and much "cleaner" than store-bought toaster waffles!

The chocolate chips are totally optional! But, one of my other little brothers tends to add chocolate to everything. So, if you have any chocolate lovers in your home, sprinkle chocolate chips into the batter to make this breakfast plate more enticing!

In a medium bowl, mix the almond milk, maple syrup, melted vegan butter, vanilla and baking powder until combined. Add the all-purpose flour and protein powder and mix again until well combined. Fold in the chocolate chips.

Spoon the batter into a greased 4-inch (10-cm) waffle iron. Cook for 2 to 3 minutes, or until the waffles are golden brown. Repeat with the remaining batter.

Enjoy immediately or allow them to cool and freeze them to toast later for a quick morning breakfast! To store in the freezer, place them in a plastic bag or container and use parchment paper to keep them separated so they don't stick together. They should last in your freezer for up to 3 months. Reheat the waffles by toasting or microwaving them.

HEALTHY TIPS: Serving these with nut butter or nondairy yogurt will help with satiety! Consider these options instead of maple syrup to help stabilize energy levels and keep you fuller longer.

Want to make these even healthier? Swap the regular flour for 1¼ cups (150 g) of oat flour! This will only add about 10 calories per waffle.

YIELD: 16 waffles

NUTRITION INFORMATION PER WAFFLE
CALORIES: 72
FATS: 2 g
CARBS: 12 g
PROTEIN: 2 g

1¼ cups (300 ml) plain unsweetened almond milk

1 tbsp (15 ml) maple syrup

1 tbsp (15 ml) melted vegan butter

1 tsp vanilla extract

2 tsp (9 g) baking powder

1 cup (125 g) regular or gluten-free all-purpose flour

2 tbsp (20 g) vegan plain or vanilla-flavored protein powder

½ cup (84 g) chocolate chips, plus more for topping

YIELD: 15 pancakes

NUTRITION INFORMATION
PER PANCAKE
CALORIES: 47
FAT: 1 g
CARBS: 9 g
PROTEIN: 1 g

1 overripe banana

1 cup (240 ml) plain unsweetened almond milk

1 tbsp (15 ml) maple syrup, plus more for serving

4 tsp (18 g) baking powder

1 tsp vanilla extract

½ tsp cinnamon, optional

1 cup (125 g) regular or gluten-free all-purpose flour

1 cup (148 g) blueberries

1 tbsp (14 g) vegan butter

Sliced bananas, for serving, optional

MAMA'S BLUEBERRY BANANA PANCAKES

Nothing says wholesome like a golden stack of pancakes for breakfast. One of my favorite childhood memories is my mom whipping up a batch of pancakes for my little brother and I on the weekends. This is a "veganized" version of a breakfast staple that I grew up loving. To make these even more nutrient dense, I've added blueberries and bananas. These pancakes are great served fresh from the skillet or made in advance and frozen for quick microwaveable pancake breakfasts.

In a mixing bowl, use a fork to mash the overripe banana. Mix in the almond milk, maple syrup, baking powder, vanilla and cinnamon (if using). When the mixture is well combined, add the flour and mix again. The batter may be slightly lumpy, which is okay. Fold in the blueberries.

Warm a skillet over medium heat and add the vegan butter. When the vegan butter is melted and begins to bubble, scoop in 3 to 4 tablespoons (45 to 60 ml) of the batter per pancake. Cook the pancakes until bubbles form on the top, then flip with a spatula. They should be golden brown on each side.

If you notice that your skillet gets too hot and the butter browns when it hits the pan, use my mama's trick and carefully remove the skillet from the heat and run it under tap water to cool it down. Do this carefully as steam will come off the pan. Allow the pan to cool for 1 minute before returning to the heat. You may also reduce the heat to medium-low to keep the pancakes from browning too much.

Serve immediately, drizzled with maple syrup and an optional topping of sliced bananas.

To store the pancakes in the freezer, place them in a plastic bag or container and use parchment paper to keep them separate so they don't stick together. These pancakes will last in the freezer for up to 3 months.

HEALTHY TIP: Want to cut back on the butter used for frying in this recipe? Use non-stick olive oil, avocado oil or coconut oil spray instead!

ALMOND & CHIA SUPERFOOD PANCAKES

Who says pancakes can't be healthy? If you're like me, and wake up craving a golden stack of goodness but want something that is going to make you feel as good as it tastes, these pancakes are for you! They have minimal carbs, are balanced with healthy fats and protein from the chia seeds and almond flour, and are super filling and fiber filled thanks to the oats.

In a medium-sized mixing bowl, stir together the mashed banana, almond milk, baking powder, vanilla, chia seeds, maple syrup and cinnamon. Then, add the almond flour and oat flour and mix until a batter forms.

Warm a skillet sprayed with olive oil, avocado oil or coconut oil spray over medium heat. When the pan is hot, spoon about ⅓ cup (80 ml) of the pancake batter into the pan. Cook for about 2 minutes (or until bubbles form on top of the pancake), then flip. Cook until golden on each side then remove from the skillet. Repeat with the remaining pancake batter.

Serve the pancakes with maple syrup, nut butter or topped with fruit.

HEALTHY TIP: Serving these with nut butter or nondairy yogurt will help with satiety! Consider these options instead of maple syrup to help stabilize energy levels and keep you fuller longer.

YIELD: 8 large pancakes

NUTRITION INFORMATION PER PANCAKE
CALORIES: 94
FAT: 4 g
CARBS: 12 g
PROTEIN: 3 g

1 mashed overripe banana

¾ cup (180 ml) plain unsweetened almond milk

2 tsp (9 g) baking powder

1 tsp vanilla extract

2 tbsp (24 g) chia seeds

1 tbsp (15 ml) maple syrup, plus more for serving

½ tsp cinnamon

¾ cup (70 g) almond flour

¾ cup (90 g) oat flour

Olive oil, avocado oil or coconut oil spray, for greasing

Nut butter, for serving

Your favorite fruit, for serving

NUTRITION INFORMATION
PER WAFFLE
CALORIES: 436
FAT: 6 g
CARBS: 82 g
PROTEIN: 12 g

1¼ cups (300 ml) plain unsweetened oat or almond milk

2 tbsp (12 g) flaxseed meal

1 tbsp (15 ml) maple syrup, plus more for serving

3 tsp (13 g) baking powder

1 tsp vanilla extract

1 cup (125 g) regular or gluten-free all-purpose flour

½ cup (45 g) rolled oats, gluten-free if needed

1 cup (166 g) diced strawberries

Olive oil, avocado oil or coconut oil spray, for greasing

Vegan butter, for serving

Fresh berries for topping

Nut butter, for serving

HEALTHY OATMEAL STRAWBERRY WAFFLES

Strawberries will brighten up any dish. They give an added pop of color, flavor and vitamin C and are the perfect low-cal add-in for these healthy and filling oatmeal waffles. This recipe is so simple and I bet you already have everything you need on hand to make them! Make these to enjoy immediately, drizzled with maple syrup and/or spread with vegan butter. Or, you can make them ahead of time and freeze to toast or microwave them on a busy morning.

In a medium mixing bowl, stir together the oat milk, flaxseed meal, maple syrup, baking powder and vanilla. Add the flour and oats and mix until a waffle batter forms. Add the strawberries and fold them into the batter.

Set a waffle iron on medium-high heat. Spray it with olive oil, avocado oil or coconut oil spray. Spoon in 2 to 3 tablespoons (30 to 45 ml) of the waffle batter and close the iron. Cook for 2 to 3 minutes, or until the waffle is golden on each side and lifts easily out of the waffle iron. Repeat with the remaining batter.

Serve with vegan butter, fresh berries, maple syrup or nut butter for a delicious plant-based breakfast that will keep you full all morning!

To store for a make-ahead breakfast, allow the waffles to cool completely before freezing them. These delicious waffles will keep in your freezer for about 3 months. Reheat them in the toaster oven or microwave and serve warm.

OATMEAL APPLE SKILLET CAKES OR MUFFINS

This recipe is the best combination of healthy, fun, filling and delicious. Can't decide if you're craving muffins or pancakes? You can use this recipe to make both! Combine your ingredients in a bowl and then make the decision of whether to bake the batter in muffin tins or fry in a skillet. Honestly, you can't go wrong with either choice! You're going to love these and you're going to love the way you feel after eating them even more!

YIELD: 9 (1-muffin or 1-skillet cake) servings

NUTRITION INFORMATION PER SERVING (NOT INCLUDING OPTIONAL TOPPINGS OR BUTTER USED FOR FRYING)

CALORIES: 111

FAT: 3 g

CARBS: 18 g

PROTEIN: 2 g

If you're making muffins, preheat the oven to 350°F (175°C) and line nine muffin tins with paper liners.

In a medium mixing bowl, mix the almond milk, maple syrup, unsweetened applesauce, melted vegan butter, vanilla, baking powder and cinnamon until combined. Then, mix in the quick oats and flour to form a thick batter. Fold in the diced apples.

Spoon the batter into the lined muffin tins and bake for 25 to 30 minutes, or until the muffins are golden brown. Remove them from the oven and allow them to cool for 2 to 3 minutes before removing them from the muffin pan. Serve warm, spread with vegan butter or nut butter.

If you're making skillet cakes, melt 1 tablespoon (14 g) of vegan butter in a skillet over medium heat. When the butter is warm and begins to sizzle, spoon about ¼ cup (60 ml) of the batter into the skillet and cook for 1 to 2 minutes, until golden on the bottom. Use a spatula to flip the skillet cake and cook for another 1 to 2 minutes, or until golden on both sides. Remove from the skillet and repeat with the remaining batter.

Serve the pancakes with nut butter or maple syrup.

You may also allow the muffins or pancakes to cool completely before storing them in an airtight container and freezing. Reheat in the microwave and enjoy them on a busy morning!

1 cup (240 ml) plain unsweetened almond or oat milk

3 tbsp (45 ml) maple syrup

½ cup (120 ml) unsweetened applesauce

2 tbsp (30 ml) melted vegan butter or coconut oil, plus more for frying or topping

1 tsp vanilla extract

1½ tsp (7 g) baking powder

1 tsp cinnamon

2 cups (180 g) gluten-free quick oats

¼ cup (31 g) regular or gluten-free all-purpose flour or oat flour

1 cup (125 g) diced Honeycrisp apples

Nut butter, for serving

Maple syrup, for serving

NUTRITION INFORMATION
PER PANCAKE WITH SYRUP
CALORIES: 84
FAT: 3 g
CARBS: 12 g
PROTEIN: 2 g

PEANUT BUTTER PANCAKES

2 mashed overripe bananas

1½ cups (360 ml) plain unsweetened almond milk

1 tsp cinnamon

1 tsp vanilla extract

4 tsp (18 g) baking powder

1 cup (125 g) regular or gluten-free all-purpose flour

1 cup (90 g) gluten-free quick oats

¼ cup (30 g) walnuts, optional, nutrition will vary

¼ cup (42 g) chocolate chips, optional, nutrition will vary

Vegan butter for frying

PEANUT BUTTER MAPLE SYRUP

¼ cup (24 g) peanut butter powder or creamy peanut butter

¼ cup (60 ml) maple syrup

PEANUT BUTTER BANANA PANCAKES

I bet these would be Elvis's favorite recipe! The classic combo of peanut butter and bananas comes together to make one of the most delectable recipes in this cookbook. Not only do they taste delicious, but they are designed to keep you full and satiated thanks to the oats, bananas and nut butters (hitting all of our macronutrients here!). If you're a peanut butter lover like me, you are definitely going to want to give these a try!

In a medium-sized mixing bowl, mash the overripe bananas and almond milk together. Add the cinnamon, vanilla and baking powder and mix. Whisk in the flour and the oats until a thick batter forms. Stir in the walnuts and chocolate chips (if using).

Heat a large skillet over medium heat and add about 1 tablespoon (14 g) of vegan butter. When the butter is melted and begins to sizzle, pour in 2 to 3 tablespoons (30 to 45 ml) of batter per pancake. Cook for 1 to 2 minutes, or until bubbles form on the tops of the pancakes and then use a spatula to flip. Cook the pancakes until golden on each side and then remove them from the pan.

Repeat with the remaining batter.

While the pancakes are cooking, make the Peanut Butter Maple Syrup. Mix together the peanut butter and maple syrup.

To serve, drizzle the Peanut Butter Maple Syrup over the pancakes and enjoy warm.

6-INGREDIENT BANANA BREAD FRENCH TOAST

Traditional French toast is made with heavy cream and eggs, is not low calorie and is definitely not vegan! But, this recipe allows you to enjoy a plate of better-for-you French toast that's free of any animal products. You only need 15 minutes and about 6 ingredients that I bet you already have on hand. This recipe is delicious! Everyone is going to love it and no one will miss the eggs and cream.

In a medium bowl, mash the overripe bananas until they have a texture similar to applesauce. Whisk in the oat milk, cinnamon and vanilla.

Heat a large skillet over medium heat and add a pat of vegan butter or spray the pan generously with cooking spray. When the butter is melted and sizzling, dip two or three slices of bread (depending on how large your skillet is) into the banana custard. When the bread is evenly coated, place it in the warm skillet and fry for 1 to 2 minutes, or until golden on the bottom. Use a spatula to flip the bread and fry for another 1 minute, until golden.

Use the spatula to remove the French toast from the pan and set it on a wire rack to cool. Continue soaking then frying the bread in the vegan butter or cooking spray (adding more as needed) until all the bread and French toast custard is used.

Serve warm topped with berries, nondairy yogurt, nut butter, banana slices or drizzled with maple syrup.

HEALTHY TIP: No bananas? No problem! Use ½ cup (120 ml) of plain non-dairy yogurt instead of the 2 bananas. This option adds about 15 calories.

No non-dairy yogurt? No problem! Use flax eggs! Mix 2 tbsp (10 g) of ground flax seeds with 4 tbsp (60 ml) of hot water. Set aside for 2 minutes until a gel forms and use this instead of the bananas. This option adds about 30 calories.

YIELD: 16 slices

NUTRITION INFORMATION PER SLICE (NOT INCLUDING OPTIONAL TOPPINGS)
CALORIES: 108
FAT: 2 g
CARBS: 18 g
PROTEIN: 2 g

2 overripe mashed bananas

1 cup (240 ml) plain unsweetened oat or almond milk

1–2 tsp (3–5 g) cinnamon

2 tsp (10 ml) vanilla extract

Vegan butter or avocado oil, coconut oil or olive oil cooking spray, for frying

16 slices vegan or gluten-free bread, preferably close to expiration date

Berries, for serving

Nondairy yogurt, for serving

Nut butter, for serving

Banana slices, for serving

Maple syrup, for serving

YIELD: 12 waffles

NUTRITION INFORMATION
PER WAFFLE
CALORIES: 68
FAT: 2 g
CARBS: 11 g
PROTEIN: 1 g

1 cup (240 ml) plain unsweetened almond milk

¾ cup (180 ml) sweet potato or pumpkin puree

2 tbsp (30 ml) melted vegan butter

2 tbsp (24 g) coconut sugar, plus more for sprinkling

2 tsp (9 g) baking powder

1 tsp cinnamon, plus more for sprinkling

1 tsp vanilla extract

1 cup (125 g) regular or gluten-free all-purpose flour

Olive oil, avocado oil or coconut oil spray, for greasing

Maple syrup, for serving

SPICED SWEET POTATO WAFFLES

One of the easiest ways to add more veggies to your diet (or onto your kiddo's plates) is by sneaking them into treats! That's exactly what you will get when you try these tasty cinnamon-spiced sweet potato waffles, inspired by my sweet potato–loving little brother. The color, texture and aroma of these frying will remind you of a cozy fall morning and the taste will have you coming back for more all year round. This is a simple, healthy and fiber-filled waffle recipe that everyone in your home will love so much that they'll forget about the hidden veggie inside!

In a medium bowl, mix the almond milk, sweet potato puree, melted vegan butter, sugar, baking powder, cinnamon and vanilla. Then, mix in the flour to form a batter.

Heat a waffle iron on medium heat. Spray with olive oil, avocado oil or coconut oil spray. When hot, spoon in about 3 tablespoons (45 ml) of batter per waffle. Cook until golden on each side and serve immediately topped with maple syrup or cinnamon.

To store these waffles for later, allow the waffles to cool completely before storing them, separated by parchment paper in a plastic bag in the freezer for up to 3 months. Reheat the frozen waffles in the toaster oven or in the microwave.

HEALTHY TIP: Want to lighten these low-cal sweet potato waffles up even more? Try skipping the sugar and butter in this recipe! This healthy swap will reduce the calories by 25 calories per waffle!

Want to make these even healthier? Try using 1 cup (120 g) of oat flour and ½ cup (45 g) of quick oats instead of using the all-purpose flour in this recipe. This swap adds about 15 calories per waffle but also adds more fiber and makes them more even filling!

BETTER-FOR-YOU BREAKFAST BAKES

Some foods are meant to nourish our bodies and some are meant to nourish our souls. Some are perfect for busy weekday mornings, and some are best enjoyed as a lazy weekend splurge. The great thing about this chapter of better-for-you baked goods is that you get the best of both worlds!

From tender Amazing Marble Oatmeal Banana Bread (page 54), fluffy 150 Calorie Blueberry Muffins (page 53) to the irresistible 30-Minute Chocolate or Vanilla Protein Donuts (page 56), each delectable recipe in this chapter is made with healthier ingredients, is vegan, gluten-free friendly, low in calories and includes nutrition information to keep you on track. Enjoy these treats warm and fresh from the oven or make them ahead of time as a grab-and-go breakfast for the week ahead.

150 CALORIE BLUEBERRY MUFFINS

There's nothing better than the smell of homemade blueberry muffins with your morning cup of coffee. These vegan blueberry muffins are everything the quintessential blueberry muffin should be: warm, soft and fluffy on the inside; golden and a little crisp on the outside. Not only are they a great breakfast, but they also make the perfect afternoon snack. I baked a batch of these recently for my brother's birthday and it's safe to say . . . they were gone in minutes! Traditional blueberry muffins are made with milk, butter and loads of sugar. I've developed a better-for-you version that is vegan, gluten-free friendly, under 200 calories and will absolutely melt in your mouth! Enjoy these warm and spread with a little vegan butter.

Preheat the oven to 375°F (190°C).

Line twelve muffin cups with paper liners. Lightly spray the muffin paper with olive oil, avocado oil or coconut oil spray to keep the muffins from sticking to the liners.

In a large bowl, add the mashed banana, almond milk, vanilla, maple syrup, vegan butter, baking soda and baking powder. Mix until combined. Mix in the flour until just combined, being careful not to overmix. Gently fold in the blueberries.

Pour the batter into the lined muffin cups, filling about two-thirds of the way full.

Bake for 25 to 30 minutes, until golden. Serve the muffins warm with vegan butter.

Store in an airtight container at room temperature for 3 to 5 days or wrap them in freezer wrap and store in a plastic bag in the freezer. Refrigeration can dry out many baked goods so I don't recommend refrigerating them.

YIELD: 12 muffins

NUTRITION INFORMATION PER MUFFIN
CALORIES: 150
FAT: 5 g
CARBS: 24 g
PROTEIN: 2 g

Olive oil, avocado oil or coconut oil spray, for greasing

1 mashed overripe banana

1 cup (240 ml) plain unsweetened almond or oat milk

1 tsp vanilla extract

½ cup (120 ml) maple syrup

5 tbsp (75 ml) melted vegan butter

½ tsp baking soda

1½ tsp (7 g) baking powder

1½ cups (188 g) regular or gluten-free all-purpose flour

1 cup (140 g) frozen wild blueberries

YIELD: 12 slices

NUTRITION INFORMATION PER SLICE
CALORIES: 199
FAT: 5 g
CARBS: 37 g
PROTEIN: 3 g

Olive oil, avocado oil or coconut oil spray, for greasing

3 mashed overripe bananas

1 cup (240 ml) plain unsweetened almond milk

¾ cup (180 ml) maple syrup (see Healthy Tips)

¼ cup (60 ml) melted vegan butter

1 tsp vanilla extract

1 tsp cinnamon

2 tsp (9 g) baking powder

1 tsp baking soda

1 cup (90 g) quick oats, gluten-free if needed

1½ cups (188 g) regular or gluten-free all-purpose flour

2 tbsp (11 g) cocoa powder (see Healthy Tips)

Banana slices, for topping

AMAZING MARBLE OATMEAL BANANA BREAD

Words cannot express how *good* this banana bread is and how impressed everyone will be when you bake a batch. It looks almost too good to eat, but it's deceptively simple and has some healthy hidden ingredients inside! It's free of white sugar, uses minimal oil and includes overripe bananas and maple syrup for sweetness and moisture. We substitute some of the flour for oats in this recipe, making it much more filling while giving it a light and fluffy texture. Bake this loaf for your family and be prepared for everyone to be amazed!

Preheat the oven to 375°F (190°C). Grease a 5 x 9-inch (13 x 23-cm) loaf pan with olive oil, avocado oil or coconut oil spray.

In a large mixing bowl, mix together the mashed bananas, almond milk, maple syrup, vegan butter, vanilla, cinnamon, baking powder and baking soda. Then, add the quick oats and flour and mix until smooth. Spoon half of the batter into the greased loaf pan.

Add the cocoa powder to the remaining batter and mix until smooth. Use a tablespoon to spoon the cocoa banana bread batter down the top-center of the regular banana bread batter. Top the batter with banana slices and bake for 40 to 50 minutes, or until golden brown and a toothpick inserted in the center of the bread comes out clean.

Store any leftover banana bread at room temperature wrapped in plastic or sealed tightly with aluminum foil.

HEALTHY TIPS: You can leave out the cocoa powder to make classic oatmeal banana bread.

If you reduce the maple syrup to ½ cup (120 ml), you will cut back on a few grams of sugar and save about 20 calories per slice.

Olive oil, avocado oil or coconut oil spray, for greasing

VANILLA DONUTS

1¼ cups (300 ml) plain unsweetened almond milk

¼ cup (60 ml) melted vegan butter

½ cup–1 cup (96–192 g) organic cane sugar (see Healthy Tips)

1 tsp baking soda

1½ tsp (7 g) baking powder

1 tsp vanilla extract

2 scoops (4 tbsp [40 g]) vegan vanilla-flavored protein powder

1½ cups (188 g) regular or gluten-free all-purpose flour
Sprinkles, for serving

CHOCOLATE DONUTS

1⅓ cups (320 ml) plain unsweetened almond milk

¼ cup (60 ml) melted vegan butter

½ –1 cup (96–192 g) organic cane sugar (see Healthy Tips)

1 tsp baking soda

1½ tsp (7 g) baking powder

1 tsp vanilla extract

½ cup (44 g) vegan chocolate protein powder or cocoa powder

1½ cups (188 g) regular or gluten-free all-purpose flour
Sprinkles, for serving

30-MINUTE CHOCOLATE OR VANILLA PROTEIN DONUTS

I couldn't write a healthy breakfast book without including one of my favorite healthier breakfast sweets! When my little brother was working out a lot, he used to mix protein powder into everything. He was on to something! Protein is so important for weight management and it can keep you feeling fuller longer. These healthier protein donuts are inspired by my protein-loving little brother who also happens to have a sweet tooth! If you're searching for a healthier, lower calorie donut that tastes just as good as a donut you can get from a bakery, give this recipe a try!

Are you a chocolate or a vanilla lover? Make either of the versions using the instructions below. Then, choose between vanilla or chocolate frosting for an added sweet treat!

Preheat the oven to 350°F (175°C). Spray twelve silicone donut molds with olive oil, avocado oil or coconut oil spray.

To make the Vanilla Donuts, in a large mixing bowl, stir the almond milk, melted vegan butter, sugar, baking soda, baking powder and vanilla. Then, whisk in the protein powder until the mixture is smooth. Mix in the flour until smooth, being careful not to overmix the batter after adding the flour or the donuts will become dense.

Or, to make the Chocolate Donuts, in a large mixing bowl, stir the almond milk, melted vegan butter, sugar, baking soda, baking powder and vanilla. Then, whisk in the chocolate protein powder until the mixture is smooth. Mix in the flour until smooth, being careful not to overmix the batter after adding the flour or the donuts will become dense.

Whichever batter you have made, spoon it into the greased silicone donut molds. Bake for 25 minutes.

VANILLA PROTEIN FROSTING, ADDS ABOUT 10 CALORIES PER DONUT

2 scoops (4 tbsp [40 g]) vegan vanilla flavored protein powder

4 tbsp (60 ml) plain unsweetened almond milk

4 tbsp (60 ml) plain unsweetened nondairy yogurt

CHOCOLATE PROTEIN FROSTING, ADDS ABOUT 10 CALORIES PER DONUT

2 scoops (4 tbsp [40 g]) vegan chocolate flavored protein powder

4 tbsp (60 ml) plain unsweetened almond milk

4 tbsp (60 ml) plain unsweetened nondairy yogurt

HEALTHY TIPS: Use as little as ½ cup (100 g) of sugar in the donuts to reduce the calories and carbs!

When shopping for plant-based protein powder, look for brands that contain little to no added sugar, dyes or other additives. Also, you may want to watch out for mentions of "natural flavors" as many studies show "natural flavors" can actually contain preservatives and other unhealthy chemicals. I like using pea protein and try to find brands that include only two to three ingredients on the nutrition label.

While the donuts are baking, make your choice of frosting. For either frosting flavor, use a whisk or fork to mix the vanilla or chocolate protein powder, almond milk and yogurt. Add more almond milk as needed, for thinner consistency. Set aside.

Remove the donuts from the molds and allow them to cool before frosting and topping with your favorite sprinkles.

YIELD: 12 rolls

NUTRITION INFORMATION PER ROLL (NOT INCLUDING MAPLE GLAZE OR CREAM CHEESE ICING)
CALORIES: 225
FAT: 12 g
CARBS: 25 g
PROTEIN: 3 g

DOUGH

1 cup (240 ml) warm (not hot) plain unsweetened almond milk

¼ cup (60 ml) melted vegan butter

2 tbsp (30 ml) maple syrup

¼ tsp salt

1 tbsp (12 g) active dry yeast

2⅛ cups (313 g) regular all-purpose flour or 2 cups (250 g) gluten-free flour, plus more for rolling

1–2 tbsp (15–30 ml) plain unsweetened nondairy yogurt, only needed if making gluten-free rolls

MAPLE PECAN CINNAMON ROLLS TWO WAYS

Whenever anyone asks me what my favorite breakfast food is, without a doubt, my answer is always cinnamon rolls. I couldn't write a vegan breakfast cookbook without including my favorite breakfast pastry! Part of living your healthiest and happiest life is balance. And, while the majority of this cookbook is full of healthy and nutritious recipes, I think it's equally as healthy to enjoy the occasional indulgent treat.

Traditional cinnamon rolls are high in calories and dairy, but these are under 400 calories, frosted and dairy free. But, no one will be able to tell! I've included two versions of this recipe: one with yeast, one without. The yeasted version takes more time and the results are worth the wait! The ones without yeast are great for a quick 30-minute cinnamon roll. Both are delicious! If you are gluten free, I recommend using the non-yeasted version. You also get the choice of either maple butter glaze or vegan cream cheese frosting.

YEASTED MAPLE CINNAMON ROLLS

To make the dough, in a medium bowl, mix the warm almond milk, melted vegan butter, maple syrup and salt. Sprinkle the active dry yeast evenly across the top of the mixture, stir gently and let the mixture sit for about 10 minutes.

Then, if using all-purpose flour, add it to the mixture and stir until a dough forms. If using gluten-free flour, stir in the flour then add 1 tablespoon (15 ml) of the nondairy yogurt and work it into the dough using your hands. If the gluten-free dough holds together and is able to be formed into a mound easily, move on to the next step. If the dough still seems dry and crumbly, add another 1 tablespoon (15 ml) of nondairy yogurt and work it in.

Leaving the dough in the bowl, form it into a mound and cover the bowl with plastic wrap or a kitchen towel. Allow the dough to sit for 1 hour. I like to place the bowl on top of an oven preheated to 350°F (175°C). The warmth from the oven helps the dough rise faster. Note, if using gluten-free all-purpose flour, the dough will not rise as much.

MAPLE GLAZE, ADDS UP TO 34 CALORIES PER ROLL

4 tbsp (60 ml) maple syrup

2 tbsp (30 ml) melted vegan butter

CREAM CHEESE ICING, ADDS UP TO 125 CALORIES PER ROLL

4 tbsp (56 g) softened vegan butter

4 oz (113 g) vegan cream cheese

1½ cups (180 g) powdered sugar

FILLING

⅓ cup (75 g) softened vegan butter

⅓ cup (63 g) organic coconut sugar or brown sugar

⅓ cup (36 g) chopped pecans

1 heaping tbsp (9 g) cinnamon

Olive oil, avocado oil or coconut oil spray, for greasing

While waiting for the dough to rise, prepare the Maple Glaze or the Cream Cheese Icing. To make the Maple Glaze, in a small bowl, mix the maple syrup and melted vegan butter. Set the glaze aside. To make the Cream Cheese Icing, in a medium bowl, using a hand mixer or whisk, combine the vegan butter, vegan cream cheese and powdered sugar until smooth.

After the dough has risen for 1 hour, place it on a floured surface and roll the dough into a ¼-inch (6-mm)-thick oval or rectangle (add more flour if the dough is too sticky to roll). Note, if using gluten-free flour, the dough will be slightly drier. Top with the filling ingredients, starting by spreading the softened vegan butter on the dough. Sprinkle with the coconut sugar, pecans and cinnamon.

Preheat the oven to 350°F (175°C). Grease a 10-inch (25-cm) or 12-inch (30-cm) round pan with olive oil, avocado oil or coconut oil spray.

Starting on the long side of the rectangle, roll the dough into a log then cut it into 12 pinwheels. Place the pinwheels in the greased baking dish so that they are close but not touching. Cover them with a towel or loose plastic wrap and set aside for another 30 minutes. Note, if your rolls are gluten free, they won't rise as much as rolls with gluten in them, but they'll be every bit as delicious!

After allowing the rolls to rise, bake them for 30 to 35 minutes, until they are golden on top.

Allow the rolls to cool before either pouring the Maple Glaze over the rolls, or spreading them with the Cream Cheese Icing.

30-MINUTE NO-YEAST RECIPE

Preheat the oven to 400°F (205°C). Grease an 8-inch (20-cm) or 10-inch (25-cm) round baking dish with olive oil, avocado oil or coconut oil spray.

In a large mixing bowl, mix the almond milk, maple syrup, coconut oil and baking powder to combine. Add the flour. Mix until a thick dough forms. If using gluten-free flour, add 1 tablespoon (15 ml) of the nondairy yogurt and work it into the dough using your hands. If the gluten-free dough holds together and is able to be formed into a mound easily, move on to the next step. If the dough still seems dry and crumbly, add another 1 tablespoon (15 ml) of nondairy yogurt and use your hands to work it in.

Transfer the dough to a floured surface and use a rolling pin to roll it into a ¼-inch (6-mm)-thick slab. Spread the slab with the filling ingredients, starting with the softened vegan butter then sprinkle with the pecans, cinnamon and brown sugar.

Starting on the long side of the rectangle, roll the dough into a log and then slice into ten pinwheels. Place each pinwheel into the greased baking dish so that they are close together with very little room between them. Bake in the oven for 15 to 17 minutes, or until golden brown. If you would like them to have more color, broil them for 1 to 2 minutes at the end of the baking time.

Allow the rolls to cool before either pouring the Maple Glaze over the rolls, or spreading them with the Cream Cheese Icing.

YIELD: 10 rolls

NUTRITION INFORMATION PER ROLL (NOT INCLUDING MAPLE GLAZE OR CREAM CHEESE ICING)
CALORIES: 259
FAT: 15 g
CARBS: 27 g
PROTEIN: 4 g

Olive oil, avocado oil or coconut oil spray, for greasing

DOUGH

1 cup (240 ml) warm plain unsweetened almond milk

2 tbsp (30 ml) maple syrup

¼ cup (60 ml) coconut oil or melted vegan butter

1½ tsp (7 g) baking powder

2¼ cups (281 g) regular or gluten-free all-purpose flour, plus more for rolling

1–2 tbsp (15–30 ml) nondairy yogurt, only use if using gluten-free flour

1 batch Maple Glaze or Cream Cheese Icing (page 59)

FILLING

¼ cup (57 g) vegan butter, softened

½ cup (55 g) chopped pecans

1 heaping tbsp (9 g) cinnamon

¼ cup (55 g) brown or coconut sugar

YIELD: 8 (1-cup [250-g]) servings

NUTRITION INFORMATION PER SERVING
CALORIES: 234
FAT: 7 g
CARBS: 36 g
PROTEIN: 4 g

Olive oil, avocado oil or coconut oil spray, for greasing

2 overripe bananas, mashed

1 cup (240 ml) plain unsweetened almond or oat milk, at room temperature

¼ cup (60 ml) pure maple syrup

¼ cup (60 ml) melted vegan butter or coconut oil

1 tsp vanilla extract

1 tsp cinnamon

1 tsp baking powder

2 cups (180 g) quick oats, gluten-free if needed

⅓ cup (41 g) regular or gluten-free all-purpose flour

2 cups (280 g) fresh or frozen wild blueberries

Additional berries and sliced bananas, for topping

BANANA BERRY BAKED OATMEAL

Nothing beats the satisfying texture of warm baked oats. This batch of buttery golden oatmeal goodness, sweetened with maple syrup and flavored with bananas, vanilla and cinnamon is divine! Many of my loved ones make my baked oatmeal recipes as meal-prepped breakfasts because of how well they refrigerate and reheat. The best part of this recipe is that it is versatile! Swap the blueberries for any kind of berries, substitute the vegan butter with healthier coconut oil, the almond milk for creamy oat milk and more! This is a make-ahead, make-it-your-way breakfast bake that tastes as good as a dessert.

Preheat the oven to 375°F (190°C). Spray a 9 x 11–inch (23 x 28–cm) baking dish with olive oil, avocado oil or coconut oil spray.

In a medium bowl, use a fork to mix the mashed bananas, almond milk, maple syrup, melted vegan butter, vanilla, cinnamon and baking powder together. Add the quick oats and flour and mix to form a batter. Fold in the blueberries.

Pour the batter into the prepared baking dish and bake for 40 to 45 minutes, or until the oats are golden brown. If you'd like a more golden appearance, turn on the broiler for the final minute of baking.

Serve immediately, topped with berries and sliced bananas.

For a quick grab-and-go breakfast, store the dish, covered with plastic or foil, in the refrigerator for 3 to 5 days. Scoop out a portion and reheat in the microwave just before serving. My mom loves to bake this oatmeal at the beginning of the week for a quick breakfast meal prep. When reheating, she loves to add a splash of oat milk to her portion before microwaving. She sometimes serves hers drizzled with maple syrup.

EASY OATMEAL ZUCCHINI BREAD

If you've made it this far into this cookbook, you probably have picked up on the fact that I love hiding veggies in my recipes. And, I love substituting some flour with oats to help make baked goods healthier and more filling! This oatmeal zucchini bread is going to blow you away! It's everything a soft and tender slice of homemade bread should be and tastes perfect on its own or spread with a little vegan butter, drizzled with maple syrup and served warm. My mouth is watering just thinking about it!

Preheat the oven to 375°F (190°C). Grease a 5 x 9–inch (13 x 23–cm) loaf pan with olive oil, avocado oil or coconut oil spray.

In a large bowl, mix the shredded zucchini, almond milk, vegan butter, maple syrup, baking powder, baking soda, vanilla and cinnamon to combine. Then, add the quick oats and flour and mix to form a batter.

Pour the batter into the greased loaf pan and bake for 40 to 45 minutes, or until the loaf is golden and has completely risen in the center. Test the center with a toothpick to make sure it's done.

Serve warm, spread with a little vegan butter and drizzled with maple syrup. YUM!

HEALTHY TIP: No zucchini? No problem! Swap it out for three mashed bananas in this recipe!

YIELD: 12 slices

NUTRITION INFORMATION PER SLICE
CALORIES: 173
FAT: 6 g
CARBS: 28 g
PROTEIN: 3 g

Olive oil, avocado oil or coconut oil spray, for greasing

⅔ cup (150 g) shredded zucchini (see Healthy Tip)

1 cup (240 ml) room temperature plain unsweetened almond or oat milk

¼ cup (60 ml) melted vegan butter or coconut oil, plus more for serving

½ cup (120 ml) maple syrup, plus more for serving

1½ tsp (7 g) baking powder

1 tsp baking soda

1 tsp vanilla extract

¼ tsp cinnamon

1½ cups (135 g) quick oats, gluten-free if needed

1½ cups (188 g) regular or gluten-free all-purpose flour

YIELD: 16 muffins

NUTRITION INFORMATION
PER MUFFIN
CALORIES: 119
FAT: 5 g
CARBS: 18 g
PROTEIN: 2 g

APPLE CIDER DONUT MUFFINS

Enjoy the flavors of a cakey apple cider donut from the comfort of your own home and without all the unnecessary oils, sugars and preservatives that are found in many store-bought apple cider donuts! These healthier apple cider muffins are made with good-for-you ingredients like unsweetened applesauce, flaxseed meal, coconut sugar and oat flour. Because they're fiber-filled, they will keep you full longer. Plus, you won't believe how moist and light these wholesome treats are!

2 tbsp (12 g) flaxseed meal

¼ cup (60 ml) warm water

2 tbsp (30 ml) apple cider vinegar

½ cup (120 ml) unsweetened applesauce

1 tsp cinnamon

¼ cup (60 ml) coconut oil or melted vegan butter

1 cup (240 ml) room temperature plain unsweetened almond milk

1 tsp baking soda

1½ tsp (7 g) baking powder

¾ cup (48 g) coconut or cane sugar

¼ tsp salt

2 cups (240 g) oat flour, gluten-free if needed

Vegan butter, for serving

Maple syrup, for serving

Preheat the oven to 350°F (175°C). Line sixteen muffin cups with paper liners.

To make the muffins, in a small bowl mix the flaxseed meal with the warm water. Let the mixture sit for 2 minutes to form a thick paste.

In a large mixing bowl, mix the apple cider vinegar, applesauce, cinnamon, coconut oil, almond milk, baking soda, baking powder, flaxseed mixture, coconut sugar and salt to combine. Then, mix in the oat flour until the batter is silky and smooth.

Pour the batter into paper-lined muffin cups and bake for 25 minutes, until the muffins have risen, are golden brown and your kitchen smells amazing!

Serve the muffins warm. I enjoy them spread with a little vegan butter and drizzled with maple syrup.

Store any leftover muffins in an airtight container at room temperature for 3 to 5 days or wrap them in freezer wrap and store in a plastic bag in the freezer. Refrigeration can dry out many baked goods so I don't recommend refrigerating the muffins.

CRAVING CINNAMON ROLL DONUTS

One of the keys to a healthy lifestyle is balance, which is why 80 percent of the time I eat foods that nourish my body and 20 percent of the time I eat foods that nourish my soul. While these cinnamon roll donuts shouldn't be a part of your daily breakfast, they are designed to be a better-for-you and healthier donut for when the cinnamon roll or donut cravings strike!

One of my little brothers is a big fan of both cinnamon rolls and donuts. When it comes time to bake him something for a special occasion, how's a big sister to choose? Thanks to this 30-minute and one-bowl recipe, I don't have to. And, neither do you! Enjoy that rich and decadent flavor of sweet, cinnamon-spiced and cream cheese–frosted cinnamon rolls, baked into a cakey low-calorie vegan donut! This is a vegan and gluten-free friendly recipe. They are light as air and literally melt in your mouth. Serve these with coffee and drizzle them with a little vegan cream cheese frosting!

Preheat the oven to 350°F (175°C). Grease fourteen donut molds with olive oil, avocado oil or coconut oil spray.

Use a fork or whisk to mix the almond milk, vegan butter, sugar, stevia, vanilla, baking powder and baking soda. Then, add the flour and mix until a batter forms. Be careful not to overmix the batter or the donuts will be dense. Fold in the cinnamon.

Spoon the batter into the greased donut molds. Bake for 25 to 30 minutes, until the donuts have risen and are golden.

If serving with icing, use a whisk to mix the softened vegan butter, cream cheese, nondairy yogurt, vanilla and maple syrup. Allow the donuts to cool, then drizzle the icing over top.

HEALTHY TIP: No stevia? No problem! Replace the stevia with another ¼ to ½ cup (50 to 100 g) of sugar in this recipe! This will only add 20 to 40 calories per donut.

YIELD: 14 donuts

NUTRITION INFORMATION PER DONUT (NOT INCLUDING CREAM CHEESE ICING)
CALORIES: 110
FAT: 4 g
CARBS: 17 g
PROTEIN: 2 g

Olive oil, avocado oil or coconut oil spray, for greasing

DONUTS

1¼ cups (300 ml) plain unsweetened almond milk

¼ cup (60 ml) melted vegan butter or coconut oil

¼ cup (50 g) sugar

4 tsp (12 g) stevia (see Healthy Tip)

1 tsp vanilla extract

1½ tsp (7 g) baking powder

1 tsp baking soda

2 cups (250 g) regular or gluten-free all-purpose flour

1 tbsp (8 g) cinnamon

HEALTHIER VEGAN CREAM CHEESE FROSTING, ADDS ABOUT 34 CALORIES PER DONUT

2 tbsp (28 ml) softened vegan butter

2 oz (57 g) vegan cream cheese

2 tbsp (30 ml) plain unsweetened nondairy yogurt

1 tsp vanilla extract

1 tbsp (15 ml) maple syrup

NUTRITION INFORMATION
PER COOKIE
CALORIES: 147
FAT: 17 g
CARBS: 18 g
PROTEIN: 5 g

2 overripe mashed bananas

1 cup (258 g) creamy peanut butter

²⁄₃ cup (126) coconut sugar (see Healthy Tip)

½ cup (120 ml) plain unsweetened almond milk

2 tsp (10 ml) vanilla extract

1 tsp baking powder

2 cups (180 g) quick oats, gluten-free if needed

PEANUT BUTTER BANANA BREAKFAST COOKIES

Cookies . . . for breakfast? Dreams do come true! If you're a peanut butter lover, like me, you're going to love this healthier vegan and gluten-free spin on a classic peanut butter cookie. They are baked golden on the outside, soft on the inside and filled with healthy oats and far less sugar than a traditional peanut butter cookie. This recipe is so quick and simple. Serve these with a glass of ice-cold oat milk for a wholesome breakfast or snack that everyone in your home will love.

Preheat the oven to 375°F (190°C). Line a baking sheet with parchment paper.

In a medium bowl mix the mashed bananas, peanut butter, coconut sugar, almond milk, vanilla and baking powder. Then, stir in the quick oats until a thick batter forms.

Use a tablespoon (15 ml) to scoop out batter and place each on the parchment-lined baking sheet. You should have twenty cookies. Bake for 15 minutes, or until golden on the top. The cookies should slide easily off of the parchment paper.

Enjoy immediately or store in an airtight container on the counter for 3 to 5 days.

HEALTHY TIP: Swap the sugar in this recipe for ½ cup (100 g) monk fruit sweetener. This brings each cookie down to about 111 calories each!

BETTER-FOR-YOU BLUEBERRY POP-TARTS®

Pop-Tarts were practically a food group in my home growing up. My little brother and I would warm these favorite childhood treats in the toaster and enjoy them as a quick breakfast or snack. Unfortunately, those pre-packaged pastries aren't usually vegan, and they definitely aren't the most nutritious.

When I told him I was writing a breakfast and lunch cookbook, he challenged me to create a homemade pop-tart recipe that's a bit better for you! And, I can now say that I've made my brother proud!

Prepare the filling by melting the vegan butter in a saucepan over medium heat. Add the blueberries, sugar and salt, and cook until the berries are tender and soften, about 5 minutes. Stir in the flour until the sauce thickens. Remove the saucepan from the heat and set aside.

Preheat the oven to 400°F (205°C). Line a baking sheet with parchment paper.

To make the crust, in a large mixing bowl use a fork to mix the almond milk, melted vegan butter, maple syrup, almond extract, vanilla and baking powder. Then, add the flour and mix until a thick dough forms.

If using gluten-free flour, add 1 tablespoon (15 ml) of the nondairy yogurt and work it into the dough using your hands. If the gluten-free dough holds together and you can form it into a mound easily, move on to the next step. If the dough still seems dry and crumbly, add another tablespoon (15 ml) of nondairy yogurt and use your hands to work it in.

When the dough is too thick to continue to mix, use your hands to form it into a mound.

Transfer the dough to a floured surface and use a rolling pin to roll it into a ¼-inch (6-mm)-thick rectangle. Use a knife to slice the dough into twenty squares.

Transfer ten of the squares to the parchment-lined baking sheet and spoon about 2 tablespoons (30 ml) of the filling into the center of each square. Top each square with the remaining squares of dough and use your fingers to press down around the edges to seal the pastries. Then, use a fork to press down around the sealed edges to create ridges.

Bake in the oven for 20 minutes, or until the pop-tarts are golden brown.

While they bake, make the icing. Whisk the powdered sugar, softened vegan butter, almond milk and vanilla. Spoon the frosting over each cooled pop-tart and top with sprinkles.

YIELD: 10 pop-tarts

NUTRITION INFORMATION PER POP-TART (NOT INCLUDING VANILLA ICING)
CALORIES: 129
FAT: 6 g
CARBS: 18 g
PROTEIN: 2 g

FILLING

1 tbsp (14 g) vegan butter

2 cups (280 g) frozen wild blueberries

3 tbsp (36 g) coconut or cane sugar

¼ tsp salt

3 tbsp (24 g) regular or gluten-free all-purpose flour

CRUST

1 cup (240 ml) plain unsweetened almond milk

¼ cup (60 ml) melted vegan butter or coconut oil, plus more for brushing

2 tbsp (30 ml) maple syrup

1 tsp almond extract

1 tsp vanilla extract

1½ tsp (7 g) baking powder

2½ cups (312 g) regular all-purpose flour or 2 cups (250 g) of gluten-free all-purpose flour, plus more for rolling

1–2 tbsp (15–30 ml) vegan yogurt, only use if using gluten-free flour

VANILLA ICING, ADDS ABOUT 50 CALORIES PER POP-TART

½ cup (60 g) powdered sugar

1 tbsp (14 g) softened vegan butter or coconut oil

1 tbsp (15 ml) plain unsweetened almond milk

1 tsp vanilla extract

Vegan sprinkles for topping

YIELD: 12 muffins

NUTRITION INFORMATION
PER MUFFIN
CALORIES: 237
FAT: 12 g
CARBS: 33 g
PROTEIN: 4 g

Olive oil, avocado oil or coconut oil spray, for greasing

3 overripe bananas

1 cup (240 ml) plain unsweetened almond milk

¼ cup (57 g) vegan butter, plus more for serving

½ cup (120 ml) maple syrup, plus more for serving

1 tsp vanilla extract

1½ tsp (7 g) baking powder

1 tsp baking soda

1 tsp cinnamon

1 cup (90 g) quick oats, gluten-free if needed, plus more for sprinkling

1½ cups (188 g) regular or gluten-free all-purpose flour (see Healthy Tip)

1 cup (109 g) crushed walnuts or pecans, plus more for sprinkling

OATMEAL BANANA NUT MUFFINS

Banana nut muffins are a great part of a healthy and nutritious morning. This recipe is so good that you will forget that these are actually good for you. Thanks to the oats they are super filling, tender and lower in calories than traditional banana nut muffins. The bananas and maple syrup provide sweetness and moisture and the nuts provide a little more protein to keep you satisfied. Everyone in your home will love them and no one will believe they're vegan and gluten-free friendly.

Preheat the oven to 375°F (190°C). Line twelve muffin cups with paper liners. Lightly spray the liners with olive oil, avocado oil or coconut oil spray to keep the muffins from sticking to the paper.

In a large mixing bowl, use a fork to mash the overripe bananas. Add the almond milk, vegan butter, maple syrup, vanilla, baking powder, baking soda and cinnamon and mix. Then, stir in the oats and flour and mix until combined. Fold in the crushed walnuts.

Fill the lined muffin tins with muffin batter, each about two-thirds full. Sprinkle the tops of each muffin with nuts and oats. Bake for 25 to 30 minutes, or until the muffins are golden brown and a toothpick inserted in the center comes out clean.

Enjoy warm, spread with butter and/or drizzled with maple syrup. Store leftovers in an airtight container at room temperature for 3 to 5 days or wrap the muffins in freezer wrap and store in a plastic bag in the freezer. Refrigeration can dry out many baked goods so I don't recommend refrigerating these.

HEALTHY TIP: Use 2 cups (240 g) of oat flour in place of the all-purpose flour in this recipe to make these even more wholesome and nourishing!

JILLY'S HEALTHY OATMEAL BITES

I couldn't write a breakfast cookbook without including one of my all-time favorite breakfast cookie recipes! These are perfect to make ahead for busy mornings when you're on the go. They have the texture of a soft baked granola bar and the flavor of a homemade oatmeal cookie. I like to make a big batch and enjoy them for breakfast (or dessert) all week long. Simply grab a few and enjoy along with your morning coffee.

Preheat the oven to 350°F (175°C) and line a baking sheet with parchment paper.

In a small bowl, mix the flaxseed meal with the warm water. Let the mixture sit for 2 minutes to form a thick paste.

In a large bowl, mix the melted vegan butter, applesauce, maple syrup, monk fruit sweetener, almond milk, vanilla, cinnamon, baking powder and salt. Add the flaxseed mixture and stir. Add the oats and oat flour and mix until a thick batter forms. Fold in the raisins.

Scoop about a tablespoon (15 ml) of batter per cookie, then roll the dough into a ball and place on the parchment-lined baking sheet. Flatten the cookies slightly with your fingers until they are about ½ inch (1.3 cm) thick. You should have about sixty cookies.

Bake for 7 to 10 minutes. The cookies will be chewy and soft.

Store in an airtight container for 3 to 5 days or in the freezer for up to 30 days. Let them thaw for 5 minutes before serving from the freezer. These are also delicious served warm, so I sometimes reheat them in the microwave.

HEALTHY TIP: No monk fruit sweetener? No problem! Use ½ cup (96 g) of coconut or cane sugar in this recipe instead! It only adds about 10 calories per cookie.

YIELD: 60 bites

NUTRITION INFORMATION PER BITE
CALORIES: 45
FAT: 2 g
CARBS: 6 g
PROTEIN: 1 g

4 tbsp (24 g) flaxseed meal

¼ cup (60 ml) warm water

½ cup (120 ml) melted vegan butter or coconut oil

½ cup (120 ml) unsweetened applesauce

½ cup (120 ml) maple syrup

½ cup (12 g) monk fruit sweetener with erythritol (see Healthy Tip)

1 tbsp (15 ml) plain unsweetened almond milk

2 tsp (10 ml) vanilla extract

1 tsp cinnamon

1 tsp baking powder

¼ tsp salt

2 cups (180 g) quick oats, gluten-free if needed

1¾ cups (210 g) oat flour, gluten-free if needed

½ cup (73 g) raisins or chopped dates

NOT YOUR AVERAGE LUNCH MENU

This book isn't your average breakfast and lunch book and the recipes in this chapter are definitely not your average lunch plates! When I was younger, I used to dread lunch. I would never know what to pack for school or work and I never felt satisfied with the choices when dining out. If you can relate, this chapter is going to change that. Here, you will find a huge variety of plant-based, gluten-free friendly, low calorie, yet highly satisfying lunches. The recipes in this chapter will both energize you and keep you full so that you can power through the rest of your day!

In this chapter, we focus on ensuring that each plate is perfectly portioned to provide a substantial amount of volume and fiber and include each essential macronutrient. This is key to keeping your blood sugar levels stable. And, of course, we focus on flavor! From healthy Adult Lunchables (yep, that's right!) on page 97, to Tofu Scramble Tacos (page 85) to Sweet Potato Black Bean Quesadillas (page 82) and Peanut Tofu Veggie Stir-Fry (page 93), there is something in this chapter that is going to get your mouth watering and will definitely hit the spot. Gone are the dreaded "what's for lunch?" days because we have a collection of answers here to that age-old question.

15-MINUTE SESAME TEMPEH BOWL

If you've never had tempeh, get ready to fall in love. Tempeh is one of my favorite plant-based protein sources and you are about to find out why! By the look and flavor of this delicious protein-packed lunch bowl, you'd think you had slaved over the stove for hours. But, this recipe is surprisingly quick and easy to make. You need a handful of simple ingredients and about 15 minutes. Make this fresh for lunch or ahead of time as a meal prep. This is a mouthwatering meal you won't want to miss.

To make the Sesame Peanut Sauce, in a small bowl stir together the ketchup, maple syrup, coconut aminos, sriracha, sesame oil, peanut butter, onion powder and garlic powder until smooth. Set aside.

To make the Tempeh and Veggies, in a large skillet over medium heat, warm 1 tablespoon (15 ml) of the olive oil. Add the sliced tempeh and cook for about 5 minutes, stirring often, until the tempeh begins to brown, about 5 minutes. Add the broccoli and the remaining tablespoon (15 ml) of olive oil to the pan. Cook, stirring, until the broccoli is tender and lightly browned. Add the Sesame Peanut Sauce and then immediately turn off the heat. Stir until the tempeh and broccoli are evenly coated in the sauce. Remove the pan from the stove.

Serve ½ cup (93 g) of the rice with one quarter of the tempeh and broccoli mixture per serving. Top with sliced green onions and sesame seeds and enjoy immediately. You can also pack this as a meal-prepped lunch and reheat in the microwave before serving.

YIELD: 4 bowls

NUTRITION INFORMATION PER BOWL
CALORIES: 391
FAT: 17 g
CARBS: 46 g
PROTEIN: 17 g

SESAME PEANUT SAUCE
1 tbsp (15 ml) ketchup
1 tbsp (15 ml) maple syrup
¼ cup (60 ml) coconut aminos
1 tsp sriracha
1 tbsp (15 ml) sesame oil
1 tbsp (16 g) peanut butter
½ tsp onion powder
½ tsp garlic powder

TEMPEH AND VEGGIES
2 tbsp (30 ml) extra virgin olive oil, divided
1 (8-oz [226-g]) block tempeh, sliced into bite-sized pieces
4 cups (364 g) broccoli florets
2 cups (372 g) cooked white rice, for serving
Green onions, sliced, for serving
Sesame seeds, for serving

YIELD: 8 quesadillas (2 small quesadillas per serving)

NUTRITION INFORMATION PER SERVING
CALORIES: 288
FAT: 8 g
CARBS: 46 g
PROTEIN: 11 g

1 sweet potato, peeled and chopped

1 cup (240 ml) water

1 (15-oz [425-g]) can black beans, drained but not rinsed

1 cup (136 g) frozen, thawed or canned corn

2 tbsp (10 g) nutritional yeast

1 tsp chili powder

1 tsp garlic powder

1 tsp onion powder

½ tsp cumin

Salt and pepper

16 small corn tortillas

Olive oil, avocado oil or coconut oil spray, for greasing

Fresh avocadoes, sliced, or guacamole, for serving

SWEET POTATO BLACK BEAN QUESADILLAS

These quesadillas are full of fiber and flavor! Sweet potatoes are one of my favorite superfoods and when you combine them with black beans, corn and southwestern spices you end up with the perfect plant-based "no queso"-dilla filling that everyone will love. Give this healthy low-cal dish a try, I bet you won't even miss the cheese!

Bring a medium pot of water to boil over medium heat. When boiling, add the sweet potatoes and cook for 10 minutes, or until the sweet potatoes are tender.

Drain about half of the water, leaving the sweet potatoes in the remaining 1 cup (240 ml) of water. Use a potato masher to roughly mash the potatoes. There should be chunks of the sweet potato remaining. Add the black beans and mash three to five more times to break apart some of the black beans, but not all. Then, add the corn, nutritional yeast, chili powder, garlic powder, onion powder and cumin and mix to combine. Add salt and pepper to taste. Mix well.

Top eight of the small corn tortillas with the sweet potato and black bean filling using a spoon or fork to ensure that the filling is evenly distributed on each tortilla. Then, place a second tortilla on top of the filling to make a quesadilla. Set aside on a plate or baking tray.

Generously spray a medium or large skillet with olive oil, avocado oil or coconut oil spray over medium heat. Add two or three quesadillas (depending on the size of the pan) and cook for 2 to 3 minutes on each side, until golden. Allow them to cool before slicing. I recommend serving these warm with fresh avocado or guacamole.

Store leftovers in the fridge for 3 to 5 days and reheat in the microwave.

If making this as a meal prep, I recommend storing the tortillas and the sweet potato black bean filling separately. Reheat the filling in the microwave. Then, assemble and fry the quesadillas just before serving. Assembly and frying should only take a few minutes.

TOFU SCRAMBLE TACOS

These tofu scramble tacos are quickly going to become one of your favorite vegan brunches or lunches! They're as easy to make as they are delicious. Tofu is a great alternative to eggs because it is low in calories, high in plant-based protein, and when seasoned and fried just right, will remind you of a savory egg scramble. To complete this tasty and filling lunch meal, serve the tofu scramble in tortillas with your favorite taco toppings. This is a well-rounded and protein-packed meal that is going to keep you feeling healthy and satisfied.

Warm a medium skillet over medium heat. Spray the pan with olive oil, avocado oil or coconut oil spray and add the peppers and onion. Cook for 3 to 5 minutes, until the onion is translucent and the peppers begin to brown. Add the whole block of tofu to the pan and use a spatula to crumble it into bite-sized pieces (adding more olive oil spray as needed). Season the tofu with the garlic powder, cumin, chili powder and turmeric. Cook for 7 to 10 minutes, stirring frequently, until the tofu is crispy and golden.

While the tofu is cooking, make the Chipotle Yogurt Dressing. In a small bowl, mix the yogurt and chipotle hot sauce and set aside.

Serve the tofu scramble in the corn tortillas, each topped with a pinch of shredded lettuce, about 3 tablespoons (32 g) of black beans, 1 tablespoon (15 ml) of salsa and 1 to 2 tablespoons (10 to 20 g) of avocado. Then dress each taco with the Chipotle Yogurt Dressing.

HEALTHY TIP: Have you ever had mushy tofu? Not exactly a pleasant experience! To ensure that your tofu is nice and firm, press it of excess water by either using a tofu press or paper towels. If using paper towels, simply slice the block of tofu into ½ inch (1.3 cm)-thick slices and then press them with paper towels until the majority of the water they were packaged in is absorbed.

YIELD: 12 tacos (3 tacos per serving)

NUTRITION INFORMATION PER SERVING
CALORIES: 388
FAT: 20 g
CARBS: 36 g
PROTEIN: 20 g

TOFU
Olive oil, avocado oil or coconut oil spray, for greasing

1 cup (149 g) chopped bell peppers

¼ cup (40 g) chopped white, yellow or red onion

12 oz (340 g) extra-firm tofu, pressed (see Healthy Tip)

1 tsp garlic powder

1 tsp cumin

1 tsp chili powder

¼ tsp turmeric

12 small corn tortillas

1 cup (47 g) shredded lettuce

1½ cups (258 g) canned black beans, rinsed and drained

1 cup (240 ml) Corn and Black Bean Salsa (page 116 or use store-bought)

1 avocado, diced

CHIPOTLE YOGURT DRESSING
¼ cup (60 ml) nondairy yogurt

1 tbsp (15 ml) chipotle hot sauce

YIELD: 12 sandwiches

NUTRITION INFORMATION
PER SANDWICH
CALORIES: 272
FAT: 11 g
CARBS: 31 g
PROTEIN: 13 g

1 tbsp (15 ml) extra virgin olive oil

1 cup (160 g) diced onion

1 (15-oz [425-g]) can lentils, lightly rinsed and drained

1 cup (117 g) crushed walnuts

¼ cup (60 ml) ketchup

1 tbsp (15 ml) vegan Worcestershire sauce

1 tbsp (15 ml) maple syrup

¼ tsp salt

¼ tsp black pepper

⅓ cup (41 g) regular or gluten-free all-purpose flour

Olive oil, avocado oil or coconut oil spray

1 cup (113 g) shredded vegan cheese

12 vegan or gluten-free hamburger buns or English muffins

LENTIL SAUSAGE PATTY MELTS

When I was younger, and much less concerned about my waistline, I used to love grabbing fast food for breakfast or lunch. Patty melts were my jam! If you have never had a patty melt, it's essentially when a grilled cheese sandwich and a hamburger join forces. Totally not vegan, and totally not healthy. But, thanks to this recipe you can enjoy a vegan and gluten-free friendly version that is much healthier (and dare I say, more delicious!). This version uses lentils and walnuts instead of meat, but you still get that nice sweet and smoky flavor thanks to the maple syrup and Worcestershire sauce. Add the patty on top of a golden toasted bun and enjoy with some melty vegan cheese.

Warm a large skillet over medium heat and add the olive oil. When the oil is hot, add the onion and cook for about 5 minutes, until golden. Add the lentils and walnuts and cook for 5 to 7 minutes, until the walnuts are tender. Remove the skillet from the heat and stir in the ketchup, Worcestershire sauce, maple syrup, salt and pepper. Set aside until cool.

When the mixture is cool, add the flour and mix to form a thick mixture. Use your hands to shape the mixture into twelve round patties about ½ inch (1.3 cm) thick.

Warm a clean skillet over medium heat and spray it with olive oil, avocado oil or coconut oil spray. Add as many patties as can fit in the pan and cook for about 3 minutes on each side, or until golden brown. When the patties are brown, reduce the heat to medium-low and sprinkle some vegan cheese on top of each patty, then cover the skillet with a lid. Cook for 1 to 2 minutes, until the cheese is melty.

Serve the sausage patties on their own, as a side to your favorite breakfast entrée or on a vegan or gluten-free bun or English muffin.

MONGOLIAN SAUCE VEGGIE LETTUCE WRAPS

Before I went plant-based, beef and broccoli was one of my favorite meals. So, I had to develop a vegan-friendly version that would give me that same mouthwatering sweet and savory flavor. This recipe is a lightened-up version with more veggies. Because of the mushrooms and broccoli, it's got a hearty texture but without any of the guilt. Serve these "Mongolian" veggies with rice or in lettuce wraps for a filling and delicious lunch that even the meat eaters around you will want.

To make the Mongolian Sauce, in a small bowl mix the coconut aminos, maple syrup and onion powder. Set aside.

To make the Peppers and Onions, warm a skillet over medium heat and add the olive oil. When the oil is warm add the minced garlic and once it starts to sizzle, add the pepper and onion. Season with salt and pepper and cook, stirring occasionally, for 5 minutes, or until the veggies are tender and golden. Remove the skillet from the heat and scrape the veggies into a bowl, returning the skillet to the heat.

To make the Mushrooms and Broccoli, using the same skillet over medium heat, warm the olive oil, then add the broccoli and mushrooms and cook for 5 minutes, or until the broccoli is tender and the mushrooms are golden brown.

Add the Mongolian sauce to the pan then sprinkle in the cornstarch. Stir for 1 to 2 minutes, or until the sauce thickens. Remove the pan from the heat.

On a platter, serve the Mongolian Sauce Mushrooms and Broccoli with the Peppers and Onions, romaine leaves, avocado and rice. To serve, fill a romaine leaf with rice, mushrooms, broccoli, onion, pepper and avocado. Top with green onions and sesame seeds.

HEALTHY TIP: Want to add more protein? Add 1 cup (198 g) of canned lentils to the skillet along with the veggies before adding the Mongolian Sauce.

YIELD: 8 wraps (2 wraps per serving)

NUTRITION INFORMATION PER SERVING
CALORIES: 321
FAT: 9 g
CARBS: 53 g
PROTEIN: 7g

MONGOLIAN SAUCE
¼ cup (60 ml) coconut aminos or low sodium soy sauce
2 tbsp (30 ml) maple syrup
½ tsp onion powder

PEPPERS AND ONIONS
1 tbsp (15 ml) extra virgin olive oil
½ tbsp (4 g) minced garlic
1 bell pepper, thinly sliced
½ cup (80 g) onion, thinly sliced
Salt and pepper

MUSHROOMS AND BROCCOLI
½ tbsp (8 ml) extra virgin olive oil
2 cups (182 g) broccoli florets chopped into bite-sized pieces
1 cup (70 g) chopped or sliced baby bella mushrooms
1 tbsp (8 g) cornstarch

LETTUCE WRAPS
8 large romaine leaves
¼ avocado, sliced
1 cup (186 g) cooked jasmine rice
2 tbsp (6 g) green onions
1 tbsp (9 g) sesame seeds

BUFFALO CHICKPEA & POTATO TACOS

One of my favorite lunches of all time used to be buffalo chicken wraps. It was not healthy and it was definitely not vegan! When I went plant based, I discovered chickpeas. They're loaded with fiber, they're filling and they are delicious. In this recipe, we combine chickpeas with peppers and onions, and then dress them with a delicious, simple buffalo sauce. This recipe is so good and will remind you of a tasty buffalo chicken wrap but with no animal products included.

2 small potatoes, diced

2 bell peppers, diced

½ cup (80 g) yellow or white onion, diced

1 (15-oz [425-g]) can chickpeas, rinsed and drained

1 tbsp (15 ml) extra virgin olive oil

Salt and pepper

½ cup (120 ml) store-bought mild or medium hot sauce

1 tbsp (15 ml) melted vegan butter

2 tbsp (30 ml) nondairy yogurt

12 small corn tortillas, buy gluten-free if needed

½ cup (75 g) diced avocado

Preheat the oven to 400°F (205°C). Line a large baking sheet with parchment paper or aluminum foil.

Add the potatoes, peppers, onion and chickpeas to a medium bowl and drizzle them with the olive oil. Season them with salt and pepper and then spread them evenly on the parchment-lined baking sheet. Bake for 40 minutes, or until the chickpeas are golden and the potatoes are crisp, flipping them halfway through the baking time.

While the veggies bake, in a small bowl, mix the hot sauce, vegan butter and yogurt. Set aside.

When the veggies are done, pour them into a bowl and toss with about half of the buffalo sauce, leaving the rest for drizzling on top.

Serve the buffalo chickpeas in the corn tortillas. Top each tortilla with diced avocado and drizzle with more buffalo sauce.

Store leftover tortillas and buffalo chickpeas separately, then combine before eating. I recommend reheating the chickpeas in a toaster oven or microwave before serving.

PEANUT TOFU VEGGIE STIR-FRY

One taste of this peanut sauce and you're going to want to slather it on everything! In this recipe, stir-fried tofu provides lots of plant-based protein and veggies provide nutrients and fiber; then, it's all tossed with this finger-licking good peanut sauce. Served over a bed of rice, this is a lunch item that you are going to crave every day!

To make the Peanut Sauce, in a medium bowl mix the peanut butter, ketchup, soy sauce, water, maple syrup and sriracha until creamy. Set aside.

To make the Stir Fry, heat a skillet over medium heat. Add the avocado oil and when it is warm add the garlic and onion and cook until both are golden. Add the tofu and cook, stirring occasionally, until golden, about 7 minutes. Add the vegetables and cook for another 5 to 7 minutes, until the veggies are tender and warm. Turn off the heat, add the Peanut Sauce and stir until the vegetables are evenly coated.

To serve, divide the rice and stir-fry between two serving bowls and sprinkle with the sesame seeds and green onions.

HEALTHY TIP: To ensure that your tofu is nice and firm in your stir-fry, press it of excess water by either using a tofu press or paper towels. If using paper towels, simply slice the block of tofu into ½ inch (1.3 cm)-thick slices and then press them with paper towels until the majority of the water they were packaged in is absorbed.

YIELD: 2 bowls

NUTRITION INFORMATION PER BOWL
CALORIES: 225
FAT: 12 g
CARBS: 26 g
PROTEIN: 5 g

PEANUT SAUCE

2 tbsp (32 g) peanut butter

1 tbsp (15 ml) ketchup

1 tbsp (15 ml) soy sauce or coconut aminos

1 tbsp (15 ml) water

1 tbsp (15 ml) maple syrup

1 tsp sriracha

STIR-FRY

1 tbsp (15 ml) avocado or olive oil

2 cloves finely chopped garlic

¼ cup (40 g) finely chopped onion

12 oz (340 g) extra-firm tofu, pressed (see Healthy Tip) and chopped

2 cups (227 g) frozen stir-fry vegetables

2 cups (372 g) cooked white rice

Sesame seeds, for serving

Green onions, for serving

NUTRITION INFORMATION
PER SCRAMBLE (NOT
INCLUDING TOAST)
CALORIES: 195
FAT: 8 g
CARBS: 25 g
PROTEIN: 8 g

BALANCED CHICKPEA SCRAMBLE

This is one of my favorite recipes in this book because it includes healthy carbohydrates and plant protein from the chickpeas, healthy fat from extra virgin olive oil and much-needed nutrients from the veggies. All these ingredients come together into one beautifully balanced and delicious dish. These scrambled chickpeas are flavorful, filling and delicious. You'll feel amazing after eating it, and it takes minutes to make. This quick and easy plate is just the thing you need to keep your day going.

1 (15-oz [425-g]) can chickpeas, rinsed and drained

2 tbsp (10 g) nutritional yeast

½ tsp cumin

½ tsp chili powder

½ tsp garlic powder

¼ tsp turmeric

2 tbsp (30 ml) extra virgin olive oil

¼ cup (40 g) diced onion

2 cups (60 g) spinach

½ cup (75 g) sliced cherry tomatoes

Vegan or gluten free toast, optional, for serving

Salt and pepper, to taste

Roughly mash the chickpeas in a medium bowl. You should still be able to see some whole pieces. Mix the mashed chickpeas with the nutritional yeast, cumin, chili powder, garlic powder and turmeric. Set aside.

Warm a skillet over medium heat. Add the olive oil and when it is warm add the onion and cook for about 2 minutes, or until golden. Add the spinach and cook for about 1 minute, or until it is wilted. Add the tomatoes and cook for 2 to 3 minutes, or until they begin to soften and brown.

Add the chickpea mixture to the pan and use a silicone spatula to press it down so that it is evenly distributed. Cook for about 5 minutes without stirring.

After 5 minutes, use the spatula to flip and stir the chickpeas; you should see that they are beginning to brown. Continue to cook for another 5 minutes, until the chickpeas are nice and golden.

Serve the chickpea scramble on its own or over toast. Season with salt and pepper and enjoy!

THREE ADULT LUNCHABLES®

Do you remember taking prepackaged lunchables to school? These are not your average lunchables! In fact, they are way better tasting and better for you! I got this idea when my sister (a busy mom and wife) was telling me about the family-friendly lunch boxes she makes for her little ones and her husband. She's got her meal prep down to a science and now you can too!

MEDITERRANEAN STYLE

This lunchable has a Mediterranean twist! It's balanced, easy to prepare and a meal that adults and kids will both enjoy. To save time, you can use store-bought hummus.

To make the Garlic Hummus, add the chickpeas to a food processor. Add the tahini, olive oil, lemon juice, garlic, cumin, salt and pepper. Blend until smooth. If the hummus is too thick, add 1 to 2 tablespoons (15 to 30 ml) of water until it reaches your desired consistency.

To make the Crispy Chickpeas, heat a medium-sized skillet over medium heat. Add the olive oil and when it is warm, add the chickpeas and season with the garlic powder, salt and pepper. Cook, stirring frequently, for 5 to 7 minutes, or until the chickpeas are crispy and golden on the outside.

To serve, place one quarter of the Crispy Chickpeas in each box with a piece of pita, one quarter of the greens, one quarter of the cherry tomatoes, one quarter of the sliced peppers, one quarter of the sliced carrots, one quarter of the sliced cucumbers, and ¼ cup (60 ml) of the Garlic Hummus.

You will have some Garlic Hummus left over. Store it in an airtight container in the fridge for up to 4 days.

YIELDS: 4 lunchables

NUTRITION INFORMATION PER LUNCHABLE
CALORIES: 363
FAT: 16 g
CARBS: 46 g
PROTEIN: 10 g

GARLIC HUMMUS

1 (15-oz [425-g]) can chickpeas, rinsed and drained

¼ cup (60 ml) tahini

2 tbsp (30 ml) olive oil

2 tbsp (30 ml) lemon juice

1 clove garlic

½ tsp cumin

Salt and pepper, to taste

CRISPY CHICKPEAS

1 tbsp (15 ml) olive oil

1 (15-oz [425-g]) can chickpeas, rinsed and drained

¼ tsp garlic powder

Salt and pepper, to taste

FOR SERVING

4 pieces of pita, naan or gluten-free wraps

4 cups (120 g) greens of your choice, I used spinach

1 cup (150 g) sliced cherry tomatoes

2 cups (300 g) sliced bell peppers

1 cup (128 g) sliced carrots

1 cup (120 g) sliced cucumbers

NUTRITION INFORMATION
PER LUNCHABLE
CALORIES: 399
FAT: 16 g
CARBS: 58 g
PROTEIN: 11 g

PB&J STYLE

Peanut butter and jelly sandwiches are a classic meal that kids (and even adults) love. This PB&J-style lunchable is a little bit more sophisticated! We use berries instead of jelly, almond butter and almonds instead of peanut butter and pita instead of sandwich bread, keeping our calories lower. But, don't worry! This might be healthier for you, but it is just as nostalgically delicious as a classic PB&J sandwich!

½ banana, sliced

½ cup (83 g) strawberries, sliced

½ cup (74 g) blueberries

Vegan or gluten-free pita bread, whole grain bread, gluten-free bread, etc.

2 tbsp (18 g) almonds

2 tbsp (32 g) almond butter, or nut butter of choice

Place the sliced fruit in one section of your container. Add your bread of choice and nuts in separate sections of the container. Add almond butter or peanut butter to a small travel container. Store in the fridge until ready to serve.

CHICKPEA MEATBALL CAESAR SALAD WRAP STYLE

If you don't want to make chickpea meatballs, no problem! I recommend swapping them out for the Crispy Chickpeas on page 97.

To make the Vegan Caesar Dressing, bring a small saucepan of water to a boil. Add the cashews and reduce the heat to a simmer. Cook, covered, for 20 minutes, or until the cashews are tender. Strain the cashews and allow them to cool.

When the cashews are cool, add them to a food processor or blender along with the water, lemon juice, soy sauce, nutritional yeast, Dijon mustard, capers, garlic powder and salt. Blend until creamy and smooth. If it is too thick, add another 1 to 2 tablespoons (15 to 30 ml) of water to reach your desired consistency. You can store this dressing in the fridge for up to 7 days.

To make the Chickpea Meatballs, add the entire contents of the canned chickpeas (including liquid) to a food processor, along with the onion, garlic, Italian seasonings, bread crumbs, gluten-free flour, 1 tablespoon (15 ml) of the olive oil, salt and pepper. Blend until thick and well combined. If the mixture is too wet to be able to shape into meatballs, add more bread crumbs or flour (2 to 3 tablespoons [7 to 14 g] at a time).

Using a tablespoon, scoop out a heaping tablespoon (15 ml) of the mixture and roll it in your hands to form the scoops into balls. If you find that your meatballs are too dry and aren't holding together well, add 1 to 2 tablespoons (15 to 30 ml) of water or olive oil to help them hold together.

Line a plate with paper towels. Warm a skillet over medium heat and add 2 tablespoons (30 ml) of the olive oil. When the oil is warm, fry the meatballs until all of the sides are golden brown, 3 to 5 minutes per side. Remove the meatballs from the pan and set on the paper towel–lined plate to cool.

To pack one lunchable, put four meatballs in a lunchbox along with two tortillas, 2 tablespoons (30 ml) of the Vegan Caesar Dressing, 1 cup (47 g) of romaine, ¼ cup (37 g) tomatoes and 1 tablespoon (4 g) of the vegan shredded Parmesan cheese. Repeat with five other lunchboxes. Store in the fridge until ready to serve. Reheat the meatballs and tortillas separately in the microwave until warm. Serve the warm meatballs wrapped in the tortillas, topped with romaine, tomatoes, Vegan Caesar Dressing, and vegan Parmesan.

YIELD: 6 lunchables

NUTRITION INFORMATION PER LUNCHABLE
CALORIES: 394
FAT: 20 g
CARBS: 44 g
PROTEIN: 12 g

VEGAN CAESAR DRESSING
1 cup (146 g) raw cashews

½ cup (120 ml) water, plus more for thinning

2 tbsp (30 ml) lemon juice

1 tbsp (15 ml) low-sodium soy sauce or coconut aminos

1 tbsp (5 g) nutritional yeast

1 tbsp (15 ml) Dijon mustard

1 tbsp (9 g) capers

1 tsp garlic powder

½ tsp salt

CHICKPEA MEATBALLS
1 (15-oz [425-g]) can of chickpeas, including liquid

¼ cup (40 g) diced onion

1 tbsp (15 g) minced garlic

2 tsp (6 g) Italian seasonings

¼ cup (27 g) regular or gluten-free bread crumbs, plus more if needed

¼ cup (37 g) gluten-free flour

3 tbsp (45 ml) extra virgin olive oil, divided

½ tsp salt

¼ tsp pepper

WRAPS
12 regular or gluten-free tortillas

6 cups (282 g) shredded romaine

1½ cups (224 g) cherry tomatoes

⅓ cup (26 g) shredded vegan parmesan cheese

YIELD: 4 bowls

NUTRITION INFORMATION
PER BOWL
CALORIES: 398
FAT: 24 g
CARBS: 39 g
PROTEIN: 10 g

5 cloves garlic

2 tbsp (30 ml) extra virgin olive oil

1½ cups (360 ml) water, divided

1 cup (146 g) cashews

⅓ cup (80 ml) lemon juice

4 cups (480 g) cooked regular or gluten-free pasta, cooking water reserved

Salt and pepper

LUNCHTIME CREAMY LEMON GARLIC PASTA

Calling all Alfredo lovers! This creamy lemon garlic pasta is the perfect healthy and filling lunch! Traditional creamy pasta sauce is made with butter and heavy cream but this plant-based version is made healthier (and more nutrient dense) using cashews! You won't believe how silky and delicious it is!

Preheat the oven to 400°F (205°C).

Place the garlic cloves in a small cast-iron or heatproof dish. Drizzle with the olive oil and bake for 30 to 40 minutes, or until the garlic is golden. Set the garlic and oil aside.

Bring a small pot with 1 cup (240 ml) of water and cashews to a boil. Boil for 25 to 30 minutes, or until the cashews are tender. Pour the cashews and their cooking water into a blender, and add another ½ cup (120 ml) of water. Add the lemon juice, roasted garlic and its roasting oil and blend until creamy. If the sauce is too thick to blend, add ¼ cup (60 ml) of the pasta cooking water until the sauce smooth and creamy.

Toss the cooked pasta in the sauce and serve seasoned with salt and pepper. Serve immediately or store in the fridge for an easy and delicious pasta lunch!

CHICKPEA AVOCADO SALAD

If you're looking for a recipe that you can make ahead as a meal-prepped lunch or snack to enjoy all week long, this is it. This will remind you of tuna salad, but without meat or dairy! And . . . it's more delicious! It's creamy, flavorful, fiber-filled and super versatile. You'll find this salad perfect for any occasion and super satisfying.

To make the Avocado Cream Dressing, add the avocado, olive oil, water, lemon juice, garlic powder, paprika, cumin, salt and pepper to a blender. Blend until creamy, adding more water if needed.

To make the Chickpea Salad, to a mixing bowl, add the chickpeas, red and green bell pepper, celery, and green and red onion.

Drizzle the Avocado Cream Dressing over the salad. Toss until mixed well.

Serve on toast, with chips/crackers, on top of salads or on its own! Store in the fridge for up to 5 days.

YIELD: 4 salads (1¼ cups [280 g] each)

NUTRITION INFORMATION PER SALAD
CALORIES: 256
FAT: 14 g
CARBS: 28 g
PROTEIN: 6 g

AVOCADO CREAM DRESSING

1 avocado, peeled and pitted

1 tbsp (15 ml) extra virgin olive oil

¼ cup (60 ml) water, plus more for thinning

1 tbsp (15 ml) lemon juice

1 tsp garlic powder

¼ tsp paprika

½ tsp cumin

½ tsp salt

¼ tsp pepper

CHICKPEA SALAD

1½ cups (246 g) canned chickpeas, rinsed and drained

½ cup (75 g) diced red bell pepper

½ cup (75 g) diced green bell pepper

1 cup (101 g) diced celery

¼ cup (12 g) sliced green onion

⅓ cup (53 g) diced red onion

NUTRITION INFORMATION
PER BOWL
CALORIES: 388
FAT: 7 g
CARBS: 61 g
PROTEIN: 17 g

SESAME STIR-FRY

If you're craving takeout for lunch, try this healthy vegan sesame stir-fry instead! Fiber-filled veggies, protein-packed tofu and rice (our carb of choice) are tossed in creamy finger-licking good sesame sauce that you will want to drizzle on everything! Whether you have 20 minutes to whip up this dish on the spot, or prepare it ahead of time for a quick meal-prep lunch, this quick and flavorful meal is going to satisfy you all afternoon! Serve this over rice, or feel free to stir the cooked rice into the stir-fry at the end for a version of fried rice.

VEGAN SESAME SAUCE

¼ cup (60 ml) ketchup

¼ cup (60 ml) maple syrup

¼ cup (60 ml) coconut aminos or low sodium soy sauce

1 tbsp (15 ml) rice vinegar

2 tsp (10 ml) sesame oil

STIR-FRY

8 oz (226 g) extra-firm tofu, pressed and dried (see Healthy Tip)

Olive oil, avocado oil or coconut oil spray

Garlic powder to taste

Salt and pepper, to taste

1 tbsp (15 ml) olive oil

1 tbsp (14 g) minced garlic

½ cup (80 g) sliced onion

2 bell peppers, sliced

2 cups (182 g) broccoli florets, cut into bite-sized pieces

3 cups (558 g) cooked jasmine rice

To make the Vegan Sesame Sauce, in a small bowl mix the ketchup, maple syrup, coconut aminos, rice vinegar and sesame oil. Set aside.

Preheat the oven to 425°F (220°C). Line a baking sheet with parchment paper.

To make the Stir-Fry, slice the tofu into triangles that are about ½ inch (1.3 cm) thick by 1 inch (2.5 cm) wide. Spray the tofu with the olive oil spray and season with the garlic powder and salt and pepper. Bake for 10 minutes, flip, and bake for another 5 to 10 minutes, or until golden.

Warm a skillet over medium heat. Add the olive oil and when warm, add the garlic and cook for 2 minutes, until the garlic is sizzling and golden. Add the onion and peppers and cook for 2 minutes, until they begin to become golden. Add the broccoli and cook for another 2 to 3 minutes, until the veggies are tender yet still firm.

Remove the skillet from the heat and toss in the Vegan Sesame Sauce and crispy tofu. Divide the rice into four bowls and top with equal portions of the stir-fry.

HEALTHY TIP: To ensure that your tofu is nice and firm in your stir-fry, press it of excess water by either using a tofu press or paper towels. If using paper towels, simply slice the block of tofu into ½ inch (1.3 cm)-thick slices and then press them with paper towels until the majority of the water they were packaged in is absorbed.

LOADED POTATO NACHOS

Confession: In my family, we love potatoes anytime, anywhere. Whether they're in the form of a French fry, a tater tot or a chip; mashed, baked and everything in between. Potatoes aren't just for dinner or snacking, and they aren't just a side dish. This vegan friendly entrée is the star of the show. I got this idea for loaded potato nachos from my bonus mom, who gets really creative when making meals designed to feed the potato lovers in my family! This recipe is kind of like nachos, but instead of chips, you will use crispy potatoes as a base, which is healthier and more filling! Instead of meat or eggs, top with vegan eggs or tofu scramble, black beans and all of your other favorite fixings. And, if you ask my dad, no dish is complete without a little cheese so add some vegan cheese shreds on top if you choose!

Preheat the oven to 400°F (205°C). Line a baking sheet with parchment paper.

Toss the potatoes with the olive oil, and season with the salt, pepper and garlic powder. Spread the potatoes on the parchment paper–lined baking sheet and roast for 25 minutes. Use a spatula to flip the potatoes, and then return the baking sheet to the oven for another 10 to 15 minutes, until the potatoes are crisp and golden.

You may also heat the potatoes in an air fryer on 375°F (190°C) for 15 to 20 minutes.

If you plan to melt vegan cheese over your potatoes, sprinkle the cheese shreds over the potatoes, spray with olive oil spray, and return to the oven for 3 to 5 minutes.

While the cheese is melting, in a small bowl stir together the nondairy yogurt and hot sauce. Set aside until ready to serve.

Divide the potatoes among four bowls and top each bowl with about one quarter of the black beans, avocado, bell peppers, onion and a serving of vegan egg. Top with the yogurt and chipotle sauce or serve it on the side.

HEALTHY TIP: No Just Egg? No problem! Use my tofu scramble recipe from the Tofu Scramble Tacos on page 85, or the Balanced Chickpea Scramble (page 94) instead! Nutrition information will vary.

YIELD: 4 bowls

NUTRITION INFORMATION PER BOWL
CALORIES: 310
FAT: 11 g
CARBS: 47 g
PROTEIN: 7 g

ROASTED POTATOES

4 large russet potatoes, diced

2 tbsp (30 ml) extra virgin olive oil

Salt and pepper

1 tsp garlic powder

TOPPINGS

1 cup (113 g) shredded vegan Cheddar cheese

Olive oil, avocado oil or coconut oil spray

¼ cup (60 ml) plain nondairy yogurt

1 tbsp (15 ml) mild or medium chipotle hot sauce

1 (13.5-oz [383-g]) can black beans, rinsed and drained

1 cup (150 g) diced avocado

1 cup (112 g) diced bell peppers

½ cup (80 g) diced red onion or green onion

4 servings store-bought vegan eggs, I used Just Egg, adds about 70 calories to this recipe (see Healthy Tip)

MAKE-AHEAD CREAMY PESTO PASTA

Did you know you can make pesto without dairy? This balanced pasta salad is tossed in bright, garlicky and creamy pesto and is a delicious way to brighten up your day! It can easily be made ahead of time and packed to serve warm or cool on a busy day.

1 cup (146 g) raw cashews

1½ cups (360 ml) water, divided

2 cups (48 g) basil

1 clove garlic

2 tbsp (30 ml) extra virgin olive oil

1 tbsp (15 ml) lemon juice

½ cup (120 ml) water

2 cups (240 g) cooked pasta, use gluten-free if needed, cooking water reserved

¼ cup (37 g) cherry tomatoes, sliced

1 batch Crispy Chickpeas (page 97)

Bring a small or medium saucepan with the cashews and 1 cup (240 ml) of water to a boil. Boil for 25 to 30 minutes, or until the cashews are tender. Add the cashews and their cooking water to a blender. Add the basil, garlic, olive oil, lemon juice, and the ½ cup (120 ml) of water and blend until creamy. Add some reserved pasta water as needed to reach your desired creaminess.

Toss the cooked pasta in the pesto and top with the tomatoes and Crispy Chickpeas.

Enjoy warm, or store in the refrigerator in four separate containers for a quick and delicious make-ahead meal.

CHICKPEA TACO BOWL

This easy and flavorful taco bowl is going to become a go-to grab & go lunch for you! Instead of using meat in this taco bowl, we use chickpeas, which are one of the best sources of healthy plant-based carbohydrates, proteins and fiber! We flavor them with a simple and delicious taco marinade, roast them until crisp, and serve them with all the traditional taco toppings for a healthy and tasty bowl that everyone will love!

YIELD: 4 bowls

NUTRITION INFORMATION PER BOWL
CALORIES: 291
FAT: 10 g
CARBS: 49 g
PROTEIN: 12 g

Preheat the oven to 400°F (205°C).

In a medium bowl, mix the nutritional yeast, avocado oil and taco sauce. Toss the chickpeas in the sauce, season with salt and pepper and then spread evenly on a foil-lined baking sheet. Bake the chickpeas for 15 minutes, toss, then return them to the oven. Bake for another 10 minutes, until they are crisp and tender.

While the chickpeas bake, make the dressing. In a small bowl mix the yogurt and taco sauce. Set aside.

Warm a small skillet over medium heat and spray with olive oil, avocado oil or coconut oil spray. Add the corn and cook, stirring, until it's lightly golden brown, 5 to 7 minutes. Set aside.

Serve the taco bowls with one quarter of the chickpeas, tortilla chips, chopped greens, corn, onion, tomatoes, avocado and dressing in each bowl.

Serve the bowls immediately or pack for a quick and healthy lunch box! If packing, store the wet and dry ingredients separately to keep them fresh.

CHICKPEAS

2 tbsp (10 g) nutritional yeast

1 tbsp (15 ml) avocado oil

2 tbsp (30 ml) store-bought taco sauce, buffalo sauce, or mild hot sauce

1 (15-oz [425-g]) can chickpeas, rinsed and drained

Salt and pepper to taste

DRESSING

½ cup (120 ml) plain, unsweetened nondairy yogurt

¼ cup (120 ml) taco sauce, buffalo sauce or mild hot sauce

TACO BOWLS

Olive oil, avocado oil or coconut oil spray

1 cup (154 g) corn

1 cup (63 g) crushed tortilla chips

4 cups (120 g) chopped greens (I used spinach)

½ cup (80 g) diced red onion

1 cup (150 g) sliced cherry tomatoes

1 avocado, sliced

YIELD: 12 slices

NUTRITION INFORMATION
PER SLICE
CALORIES: 234
FAT: 15 g
CARBS: 20 g
PROTEIN: 6 g

CRUST

1 cup (240 ml) lukewarm water

¼ cup (60 ml) melted vegan butter or olive oil, plus more for brushing and drizzling

1 tbsp (15 ml) maple syrup or sugar

1½ tsp (7 g) baking powder

½ tsp garlic powder, optional

2 tsp (6 g) Italian seasonings, optional

¼ tsp salt

2¼ cups (281 g) regular or gluten-free all-purpose flour

PESTO

2 cups (48 g) fresh basil

¼ cup (60 ml) extra virgin olive oil

½ cup (68 g) pine nuts

2 tsp (10 ml) lemon juice

2 cloves garlic

¼ tsp salt

1–2 tbsp (15–30 ml) water

TOPPINGS

1 cup (100 g) grated vegan Parmesan cheese

½ cup (75 g) sliced tomatoes

NEW & IMPROVED PESTO PIZZA

Who says pizza can't be healthy? Who says pizza can't be vegan? Who says pizza can't be low calorie? This recipe is the answer to all three questions! This recipe includes flavorful garlicky pesto spread onto a golden and crisp crust. My first cookbook has an awesome pesto pizza recipe. But I recently created a new, even better pizza crust recipe that blew everyone away! Give my new and improved pesto pizza a try and I am sure it will leave you satisfied.

Preheat the oven to 400°F (205°C).

To make the crust, in a medium bowl mix the water, vegan butter, maple syrup, baking powder, garlic powder and Italian seasonings (if using) and salt. Then, add the flour and mix until a thick dough forms. Using your hands, form the dough into a round.

Transfer the dough to a sheet of parchment paper and roll it into a ¼-inch (6-mm)-thick slab. Slide the parchment paper and dough onto a pizza pan and brush the edges of the dough with melted vegan butter or olive oil. Bake for 12 minutes.

While the crust is baking, add the basil, olive oil, pine nuts, lemon juice, garlic cloves and salt to a food processor. Pulse on high speed until a creamy pesto forms, adding a tablespoon or two (15 to 30 ml) of water if it's too thick. Set it aside until you're ready to assemble the pizza.

Remove the crust from the oven, spread the pesto onto the crust (leaving about 1 inch [2.5 cm] of room around the edges) and then sprinkle with the vegan Parmesan. Top with the tomatoes and broil for 2 to 4 minutes, or until the cheese has melted and the pesto is browned. The edges of the crust should be golden. Watch carefully while broiling to ensure the pizza doesn't burn. Cut into twelve slices and enjoy!

PICO DE GALLO

1 cup (150 g) chopped cherry tomatoes

¼ cup (40 g) chopped red onion

Juice of 1 lime

2 tbsp (6 g) chopped green onions

2 tbsp (2 g) chopped cilantro

GUACAMOLE

2 large ripe avocados

2 tbsp (30 ml) lime juice

⅓ cup (53 g) diced red onion

⅓ cup (59 g) diced tomato

½ tsp cumin

½ tsp garlic powder

1 tsp salt

1 tbsp (1 g) sliced cilantro, optional

½ tbsp (4 g) sliced jalapeño, optional

CORN & BLACK BEAN SALSA

1 tbsp (15 ml) avocado oil

1 cup (154 g) corn, either frozen and thawed corn or canned corn, rinsed and drained

1 tsp garlic powder

½ tsp paprika

½ tsp cumin

Salt and pepper

1 tbsp (15 ml) coconut cream, optional

2 tbsp (6 g) chives or green onions

½ cup (86 g) canned black beans, rinsed and drained

THREE AMIGOS PLATE

Sometimes you want a full meal for lunch, and sometimes you want a snack you can share with friends. I call this recipe the three amigos because back in my Corporate America days, I would go to a local Mexican restaurant here in Atlanta with two of my good friends. We would order something called The Three Amigos, which describes us perfectly. It was cheese dip, guac and salsa with seasoned tortilla chips that were addictive! This is my plant-based version with my famous homemade guac, pico de gallo and corn and black bean salsa!

To make the Pico de Gallo, in a small bowl combine the tomatoes, onion, lime juice, green onions and cilantro. Mix and set aside. You can make the Pico de Gallo ahead of time and store it in the fridge for 3 to 5 days.

Next, make the Guacamole. Slice the avocados in half, peel and remove the pits. Place the avocados in a bowl. Drizzle them with the lime juice and use a fork to mash the avocado and lime juice together. Fold in the red onion and tomato then mix in the cumin, garlic powder and salt. Add the cilantro and jalapeño (if using).

Next, make the Corn & Black Bean Salsa. Warm a skillet over medium heat. Add the avocado oil and when it is warm, add the corn and season with garlic powder, paprika, cumin, salt and pepper. Cook, stirring, for 5 to 7 minutes, until the corn is lightly browned. Stir in the coconut cream (if using) and chives. Remove the skillet from the heat and fold in the black beans. The salsa can be served warm or cool.

SEASONED TORTILLA CHIPS

12 small corn tortillas

Olive oil, avocado oil or coconut oil spray

1 tsp garlic powder

½ tsp cumin

1 tsp salt

1 tsp paprika

½ tsp onion powder

Last, make the Seasoned Tortilla Chips. Preheat the oven to 425°F (220°C). Line a baking sheet with parchment paper or foil.

Slice the tortillas in half and then slice each half into three triangles. Place the tortillas on the parchment-lined baking sheet and spray the tops with olive oil, avocado oil or coconut oil spray. Sprinkle them generously (or to taste) with garlic powder, cumin, salt, paprika and onion powder and bake for 5 to 7 minutes, until crispy and browned.

Serve the tortilla chips warm alongside the Guacamole, Corn & Black Bean Salsa and Pico de Gallo.

FUEL UP GREEK HUMMUS PITA POCKETS

This fresh meal is one of the easiest recipes in my book and also one of the most delicious. It's loaded with veggies, superfoods and fiber. Use either homemade or store-bought hummus and you've got a healthy plant-based lunch that will keep your energy tank full!

YIELD: 4 pitas

NUTRITION INFORMATION
PER PITA
CALORIES: 256
FAT: 31 g
CARBS: 11 g
PROTEIN: 9 g

To prepare the Homemade Hummus, add the chickpeas, tahini, olive oil, lemon juice, garlic, cumin and salt and pepper to a food processor. Blend. Then, add the 2 tablespoons (30 ml) of water. Blend again until smooth and creamy. If it's still too thick, add 2 to 4 tablespoons (30 to 60 ml) of water and blend until you reach your desired consistency. Remember, you can always add more water but you can't take it out! Place the hummus in the fridge to cool until you are ready to serve.

To make the Pita Pockets, warm a skillet over medium heat. Add the olive oil and when warm, add the onion, bell pepper and mushrooms and cook, stirring, for 7 to 10 minutes, or until the veggies are browned.

Spread each pita with ¼ cup (60 ml) of the hummus. Then fill each pita with one quarter of the spinach, romaine, sliced tomatoes, avocado slices and the sautéed veggie mixture. Serve immediately or pack for a healthy lunch for the next day!

HOMEMADE HUMMUS

1 (15-oz [425-g]) can chickpeas, rinsed and drained

¼ cup (60 ml) tahini

2 tbsp (30 ml) extra virgin olive oil

2 tbsp (30 ml) lemon juice

1 clove garlic

½ tsp cumin

Salt and pepper, to taste

2-6 tbsp (30-90 ml) water, divided

PITA POCKETS

1 tbsp (15 ml) extra virgin olive oil

½ cup (80 g) thinly sliced onion

1 bell pepper, thinly sliced

1 cup (70 g) sliced baby bella mushrooms

4 slices vegan or gluten-free naan or pita (large tortillas also work)

1 cup (30 g) fresh spinach

1 cup (34 g) romaine

1 cup (180 g) sliced tomatoes

4 thin slices of avocado

YIELD: 4 bowls

NUTRITION INFORMATION
PER BOWL
CALORIES: 257
CARBS: 36 g
FAT: 10 g
PROTEIN: 7 g

2 tbsp (30 ml) extra virgin olive oil

1 tbsp (14 g) minced garlic

2 cups (140 g) baby bella mushrooms, chopped

2 cups (248 g) chopped zucchini

Salt and pepper, to taste

4 cups (932 g) prepared grits

¼ cup (28 g) shredded vegan Cheddar cheese

¼ cup (37 g) chopped cherry tomatoes

1 tbsp (3 g) chopped green onion

Store-bought vegan egg, I used Just Egg, adds about 70 calories per bowl (see Healthy Tip)

BRUNCH FOR LUNCH VEGGIE GRIT BOWL

I recently went to a plant-forward restaurant here in Atlanta with my family and they had some of the most delicious brunch items on their menu. There were so many options to choose from, which was exciting because as a plant-based and gluten-free eater, I hardly ever have many choices on the menu. I opted to try their savory breakfast bowl because it sounded so unique yet super healthy! It was! This veggie grit bowl is inspired by that hearty wholesome brunch. It's super filling, flavorful and will leave you feeling satisfied all afternoon.

To prepare the veggies, warm a skillet over medium heat then add the olive oil. When it is hot, add the minced garlic.

When it sizzles, add the mushrooms and zucchini and season with salt and pepper. Cook, stirring for 10 to 12 minutes, or until the veggies are golden brown.

While the veggies cook, in a seperate pot or dish, prepare the grits by warming on the stovetop or in the microwave (follow the instructions on the packaging), so that you yield 4 cups (932 g) of prepared grits.

Top the warm grits with the vegan cheese, veggie mixture, tomatoes, green onions and egg (if using). Enjoy warm.

HEALTHY TIP: Don't have vegan eggs? No problem! Use my tofu scramble recipe from the Tofu Scramble Tacos on page 85, or the Balanced Chickpea Scramble (page 94) for this delicious brunch or lunch plate! You can also top this with Crispy Chickpeas (page 97)! Nutrition information will vary.

OPEN-FACED HUMMUS SANDWICH WITH ROASTED SWEET POTATOES

YIELD: 4 sandwiches

NUTRITION INFORMATION PER SANDWICH
CALORIES: 392
FAT: 10 g
CARBS: 62 g
PROTEIN: 10 g

This open-faced sandwich is quickly going to become one of your favorite midday meals. I got the idea from my bonus mom, who told me she loves having hummus on toast for lunch! I decided to give it a go. Simply spread homemade or store-bought hummus on a slice of golden toast and top with veggies and crispy chickpeas to make this meal more substantial. Serve with a side of homemade crispy sweet potatoes and you have a fiber-filled nutritious lunch that tastes and feels like an afternoon indulgence.

2 sweet potatoes, peeled and cut into bite-sized pieces

1 tbsp (15 ml) extra virgin olive oil

1 tsp garlic powder

¼ tsp paprika

¼ tsp chili powder

½ tsp oregano

½ tsp cumin

Salt and pepper

8 slices regular, vegan, or gluten-free bread, I prefer whole grain or Ezekiel bread

1 batch Homemade Hummus (page 119)

1 batch Crispy Chickpeas (page 97)

¼ cup (37 g) sliced cherry tomatoes

1 tbsp (4 g) chopped parsley or cilantro

Preheat the oven to 400°F (205°C). Line a baking sheet with parchment paper.

Toss the sweet potatoes with the olive oil and season with the garlic powder, paprika, chili powder, oregano, cumin, salt and pepper. Spread them on the parchment-lined baking sheet and bake for 25 to 30 minutes, flipping halfway, until golden brown on the outside and tender on the inside.

When ready to serve, toast the bread if desired. Spread 2 tablespoons (30 ml) of the Homemade Hummus on each slice of toast and top each slice with 2 tablespoons (30 g) of the Crispy Chickpeas. Top with about one quarter of the tomatoes and parsley. Serve with about 1 cup (130 g) of roasted sweet potatoes.

Store any leftover sweet potatoes in a storage container in the refrigerator for up to 4 days.

PRO TIP: If you have an air fryer, you can air fry the chickpeas and sweet potatoes together at 375°F (190°C) for about 15 minutes. You can also use an air fryer to reheat the chickpeas and sweet potatoes before serving on the toast.

SUPER-FILLING SOUPS & SALADS

Are you a soup or salad person? I'm both! And, no proper lunch recipe book would be complete without an array of options for both. Here you will find nourishing and filling soups such as my famous Nourishing Sweet Potato Black Bean Chili (page 127), my dad's favorite protein-packed Caesar Salad with Crispy Chickpeas and Tempeh or Tofu (page 147), and a waistline-friendly Sassy Strawberry Quinoa Salad (page 139).

For many of us, lunch is a meal that tends to be the most challenging to plan for. We are in the midst of our busy days, often on the go, with only minutes to spare. Sure, there are fast-food restaurants, but that usually isn't the healthiest option on a daily basis. Popular soup and salad options are often high in calories, low in satiety and expensive! This chapter will help you fuel up with a filling soup or salad during your midday meal without breaking your nutrition goals or bank account!

NOURISHING SWEET POTATO BLACK BEAN CHILI

Chili is one of the best make-ahead meals. Many people don't often think of chili as a healthy meal because it's usually loaded with fatty meat and other animal products. But, this version is meat and dairy-free, super clean and nourishing. It includes healthful gut-friendly and fiber-filled ingredients like black beans, potatoes and sweet potatoes. Add spinach and peppers to pump up the veggies and top with a superfood—avocado—that's one of the healthiest fats out there!

Warm a medium saucepan over medium heat. Add the olive oil and when it is warm add the red onion and garlic and cook for 2 minutes, until fragrant. Add the potato and sweet potato and cook for 10 minutes, stirring occasionally. Add the bell peppers and cook for 5 minutes, stirring occasionally, until the veggies are tender.

Add the vegetable broth, tomato sauce, cumin, garlic powder, onion powder, paprika and black pepper to the pot. Cook, stirring occasionally, until the soup comes to a low boil. Reduce the heat to low and simmer, covered, for 20 minutes. Turn off the heat but keep the pot on the warm burner. Stir in the black beans and spinach and cover until it's time to serve.

Enjoy topped with the avocado, parsley and tortilla chips if you'd like.

YIELD: 4 bowls

NUTRITION INFORMATION PER BOWL (NOT INCLUDING TORTILLA CHIPS)
CALORIES: 311
FAT: 14 g
CARBS: 42 g
PROTEIN: 8 g

1 tbsp (15 ml) extra virgin olive oil

¾ cup (120 g) diced red onion

2 tsp (9 g) minced garlic

1 cup (150 g) chopped red or gold potato

2 cups (268 g) diced sweet potato

1 cup (149 g) diced bell peppers

2 cups (480 ml) low-sodium vegetable broth or water

½ cup (120 ml) canned tomato sauce

1½ tsp (3 g) cumin

1 tsp garlic powder

1 tsp onion powder

1 tsp paprika

½ tsp black pepper

1 (15-oz [425-g]) can black beans, rinsed and drained

4 cups (120 g) fresh spinach

1 avocado, diced

¼ cup (15 g) freshly chopped parsley

Tortilla chips, optional, for serving

YIELD: 4 salads

NUTRITION INFORMATION
PER SALAD
CALORIES: 390
FAT: 14 g
CARBS: 55 g
PROTEIN: 14 g

CHICKPEA ORANGE SALAD

Say hello to your new favorite way to enjoy a salad! By adding grains, crispy chickpeas and nuts, we elevate the flavors, nutrition content, and texture of a standard salad. This recipe is completed by the addition of a creamy orange dressing that is so mouthwatering! This orange peanut grain bowl is one of my personal favorite salads and it hits all the macronutrients we are striving for!

To make the Orange Dressing, in a small bowl whisk the orange juice, maple syrup, apple cider vinegar and nondairy yogurt (if using) until creamy and smooth. Taste test it and add 1 more tablespoon (15 ml) of maple syrup if you would like a sweeter dressing. If you want a tarter dressing, add another ½ tablespoon (8 ml) of the vinegar. Whisk again until smooth and set aside.

To plate the salads, divide the chopped kale, cabbage, cooked white rice, peanuts, salt, pepper and Crispy Chickpeas among four plates. Drizzle with the Orange Dressing and toss. Serve immediately.

If storing this salad for later, keep all of the ingredients refrigerated until ready to serve. I recommend storing the dressing on the side and drizzling it over the salad just before serving.

ORANGE DRESSING

¼ cup (60 ml) freshly squeezed orange juice

2 tbsp (30 ml) maple syrup, or more for desired sweetness

1 tbsp (15 ml) apple cider vinegar, or more for desired tartness

2 tbsp (30 ml) plain unsweetened nondairy yogurt, optional, makes it creamier

SALAD

4 cups (268 g) chopped kale

2 cups (140 g) chopped purple cabbage

2 cups (372 g) cooked white or brown rice

½ cup (73 g) roasted and salted peanuts

Salt and pepper

1 batch Crispy Chickpeas (page 97)

LOW-CAL VEGAN BAKED POTATO SOUP

If you're plant-based and missing that cozy and creamy flavor of baked potato soup, this lower calorie vegan version is for you! It's flavored to perfection, creamy and so delicious. The nutritional yeast gives this delectable dish a cheesy flavor. Did you know that nutritional yeast is also a great source of vitamin B12 (something that people who don't eat meat need to ensure we get enough of)? The liquid smoke brings it that savory and smoky flavor without any animal products! If you're craving comfort, you're going to love this dish. It's quick, easy, low calorie and guaranteed to be a crowd favorite.

Dice the potatoes into 1-inch (2.5-cm) cubes. Add the diced potatoes to a medium pot and fill with water until the potatoes are covered. Bring the water to a boil then reduce the heat to simmer and cover the pot. Simmer until the potatoes are soft, 15 to 20 minutes. When the potatoes are done, drain and set aside.

Warm a large saucepan on medium heat and add the vegan butter. When the butter has melted, add the onion and garlic. Sauté until the onion is golden but not browned (about 5 minutes), then add the boiled potatoes, vegetable broth, almond milk, nutritional yeast, liquid smoke, paprika and salt. Bring the soup to a boil. When boiling, cover and reduce the heat to simmer. Simmer for 15 minutes, covered.

Remove the pot from the heat and use an immersion blender to blend the soup.

Top with chives, vegan bacon or shredded vegan Cheddar cheese, or any of your favorite baked potato toppings!

YIELD: 2 bowls

NUTRITION INFORMATION PER BOWL
CALORIES: 268
FAT: 8 g
CARBS: 38 g
PROTEIN: 12 g

2 medium russet potatoes

1 tbsp (14 g) vegan butter

½ cup (80 g) diced yellow onion

1 tbsp (15 g) minced garlic

2 cups (480 ml) vegetable broth

½ cup (120 ml) plain unsweetened almond milk

1 tbsp (5 g) nutritional yeast

½ tsp liquid smoke or 1 tbsp (15 ml) vegan Worcestershire sauce

½ tsp paprika

½ tsp salt

Chives, for topping

Vegan bacon, for topping

Shredded vegan Cheddar cheese, for topping

YIELD: 2 bowls

NUTRITION INFORMATION
PER BOWL
CALORIES: 268
FAT: 14 g
CARBS: 30 g
PROTEIN: 8 g

1 tbsp (15 ml) extra virgin olive oil

⅓ cup (53 g) diced onion

1 clove freshly chopped garlic

1 cup (240 ml) canned tomato sauce

1 (15-oz [425-g]) can black beans, rinsed and drained

1 tsp chili powder

½ tbsp (8 g) sugar

1 tsp cumin

¼ cup (60 ml) plain, unsweetened nondairy yogurt

¼ cup (38 g) sliced avocado

⅛ cup (16 g) tortilla chips, for topping

CREAMY BLACK BEAN TOMATO SOUP

This dish combines two of my favorite Mexican soups into a super tasty bowl of deliciousness! Black bean soup and tortilla soup join forces to create this creamy, comforting and flavorful meal. Thanks to the black beans, this is a filling dish that everyone will love.

Warm a saucepan over medium heat. Add the olive oil and when warm, add the onion and garlic and cook for about 5 minutes, until golden. Add the tomato sauce, black beans, chili powder, sugar and cumin. Bring the soup to a boil then reduce the heat to low. Cover and cook for 10 minutes.

Remove the pot from the heat and use a handheld immersion blender to blend the contents of the pot. Add the nondairy yogurt and stir until creamy.

Serve immediately topped with the sliced avocado and tortilla chips.

QUINOA BLACK BEAN SALAD

This healthy lunch idea is inspired by my sweet aunt who loves to entertain and constantly has a house full of people. She's busy but manages to pull off the most delicious and healthy meals! She served a version of this a couple of years ago and even the non-vegans loved it! This recipe is so easy, healthy and delicious you will want to make it every week and especially for those busy weeks when you're on the go but need something filling and satisfying.

YIELD: 8 (1-cup [100-g]) servings

NUTRITION INFORMATION PER SERVING
CALORIES: 225
FAT: 12 g
CARBS: 26 g
PROTEIN: 6 g

Prepare the dried quinoa according to instructions on the packaging. When cooked, fluff the quinoa with a fork and let it cool, covered, for 20 minutes.

To a large bowl, add the cooled quinoa, corn, black beans, red onion, scallion, tomatoes and avocado.

In a small bowl, whisk the avocado oil, maple syrup and lime juice. Drizzle the dressing over the quinoa and veggies and toss. Season with salt and pepper and enjoy either warm or cool.

This quinoa salad tastes great with tortilla chips, on its own or as a taco filling.

1 cup (170 g) uncooked tricolor quinoa

1 cup (136 g) frozen corn, thawed and drained

1 (15-oz [425-g]) can black beans, rinsed and drained

½ red onion, diced

1 scallion, sliced

1 cup (150 g) cherry or grape tomatoes, sliced

1 avocado, diced

3 tbsp (45 ml) avocado oil

1 tbsp (15 ml) maple syrup or agave

1 tbsp (15 ml) lime juice

Salt and pepper

Tortilla chips, optional, for serving

YIELD: 4 salads

NUTRITION INFORMATION
PER SALAD
CALORIES: 260
FAT: 17 g
CARBS: 27 g
PROTEIN: 2 g

ROASTED SWEET POTATOES

2 sweet potatoes

1 tbsp (15 ml) extra virgin olive oil

1 tsp garlic powder

½ tsp paprika

Salt and pepper

MAPLE DIJON DRESSING

1 tbsp (15 ml) Dijon mustard

2 tbsp (30 ml) maple syrup

¼ cup (60 ml) extra virgin olive oil

Salt and pepper

SALAD

4 cups (268 g) chopped kale

1 Honeycrisp apple, diced

4 green onions or ¼ cup (40 g) finely chopped yellow or red onion

1 avocado, diced

½ cup (67 g) sunflower seeds or crushed walnuts

SUPERFOOD APPLE & KALE SALAD

This apple and kale salad will quickly become a regular lunchtime staple! All the nutrient-dense superfoods in this recipe will have you feeling your best all afternoon. From kale and sweet potatoes, to crisp and juicy Honeycrisp apples, to avocado, to nuts and seeds—this recipe has everything you need to feel nourished and energized!

To make the Roasted Sweet Potatoes, preheat the oven or an air fryer to 400°F (205°C). If using the oven, line a baking sheet with parchment paper.

Chop the sweet potatoes into ½-inch (1.3-cm) squares and place them in a medium mixing bowl. Drizzle them with the olive oil, then season with the garlic powder, paprika and salt and pepper to taste. Toss until evenly coated.

Spread the sweet potatoes in the bottom of an air fryer or on the parchment-lined baking sheet. Air fry or bake for 15 to 20 minutes, or until the sweet potatoes are tender and browned around the edges. Remove from the air fryer or oven and allow to cool before serving.

While the potatoes cool, make the Maple Dijon Dressing. In a small bowl, whisk the Dijon, maple syrup, olive oil, salt and pepper together until a creamy dressing forms.

To assemble the salad, place the chopped kale in a large mixing bowl. Drizzle the Maple Dijon Dressing over the kale then use your hands to massage the dressing into the kale for 2 to 3 minutes, until the kale becomes tender. Top with the diced apples, roasted sweet potatoes, green onions, avocado and sunflower seeds. Toss, divide among four plates and enjoy!

If you would like additional protein, feel free to add the protein of your choice, such as Crispy Tofu, Marinated Tempeh & Crispy Chickpeas (see my Caesar Salad with Crispy Chickpeas and Tempeh or Tofu on page 147).

SASSY STRAWBERRY QUINOA SALAD

Looking for a healthy salad for lunch that is waistline friendly and delicious? Give this super simple salad a try! It has all the macronutrients you need to power you through the afternoon: healthy carbs from the berries and cucumbers; plant protein from the quinoa, chickpeas and pumpkin seeds; and healthy fats from the homemade white balsamic dressing. Plus, it's fiber filled! This is the perfect balanced salad for busy weekdays and it travels well.

To prepare the White Balsamic Vinaigrette, in a small bowl whisk the olive oil, white balsamic vinegar and agave. Set aside.

To make the salad, warm a large skillet over medium heat. Add the olive oil and when it is warm, add the chickpeas and season with salt, pepper and garlic powder (if using). Cook, stirring often, for 7 to 10 minutes, until the chickpeas are crisp and golden. Set them aside to cool.

Add about one quarter of the spinach and kale to each of four salad bowls. Top each bowl with about one quarter of the cooked and cooled quinoa and crispy chickpeas. Add one quarter of the cucumbers, strawberries and pumpkin seeds to each bowl. Drizzle with about 2 tablespoons (30 ml) of dressing per salad and toss, and add more dressing to taste. Season with salt and pepper and enjoy.

If packing this for a to-go lunch, store with the dressing on the side until ready to serve.

YIELD: 4 salads

NUTRITION INFORMATION PER SALAD
CALORIES: 296
FAT: 19 g
CARBS: 47 g
PROTEIN: 10 g

WHITE BALSAMIC VINAIGRETTE

¼ cup (60 ml) extra virgin olive oil, plus more for chickpeas

2 tbsp (30 ml) white balsamic vinegar

1 tsp agave, add more to desired sweetness

SALAD

1 tsp extra virgin olive oil, plus more as needed

1 (15-oz [425-g]) can chickpeas, rinsed and drained

Salt and pepper to taste

½ tsp garlic powder, optional

4 cups (120 g) fresh spinach

4 cups (268 g) fresh kale leaves

1½ cups (278 g) quinoa, cooked

2 cups (266 g) sliced and quartered cucumbers

1 cup (166 g) sliced strawberries

2 tbsp (18 g) roasted pumpkin seeds

1 tbsp (14 g) vegan butter

½ cup (80 g) diced onion

2 cups (272 g) frozen corn

1 tsp garlic powder

1 tsp red pepper flakes

½ tsp chili powder

½ tsp cumin

¼ tsp salt

¼ tsp pepper

2 cups (227 g) cauliflower rice

2 cups (480 ml) vegetable broth

1 cup (240 ml) plain unsweetened almond milk

¼ cup (31 g) all-purpose flour

1 tbsp (1 g) cilantro, for serving

1 cup (150 g) sliced avocado, for serving

Vegan or gluten-free toasted bread or tortilla chips, for serving

LIGHTER CAULIFLOWER CORN CHOWDER

Ah, corn chowder. One of my guilty pleasures in life. Until now! This corn chowder is hearty, thick, creamy and surprisingly low calorie. My secret to keeping this chowder thick and hearty without going overboard on the indulgence is cauliflower. And, you won't even taste it. Seasoned to perfection, this corn chowder has a delicious and bold Tex Mex flavor. It's creamy with the perfect amount of heat. And, the hidden cauliflower is nutritious and filling.

Warm a medium saucepan over medium-high heat, then add the vegan butter and cook until melted. Add the onion and cook for 2 to 3 minutes, until golden. Add the corn, garlic powder, red pepper flakes, chili powder, cumin, salt and pepper. Cook for 3 to 5 minutes, until the corn becomes slightly browned. Then, add the cauliflower rice and cook for another 2 to 3 minutes, until the cauliflower becomes soft. Add the vegetable broth and almond milk.

Bring the soup to a boil and then remove the pot from the heat. Use a handheld immersion blender to blend soup. Sift in the flour while whisking the chowder. Whisk gently until there are no lumps.

Serve warm topped with cilantro, sliced avocado and toast.

QUICK BERRIES & TOASTED OAT SALAD

This is the perfect salad to make when you're unsure of what to make for lunch! This low-calorie lunch is perfect for those of us who love fruit on their salads and who like a little crunch in each bite. I love to mix this up quickly and enjoy it as a midday meal. The toasted oats smell and taste amazing and because the ingredients are so simple and clean, you're going to feel amazing after eating it!

Prepare the vinaigrette by adding the olive oil, white wine vinegar, maple syrup and Dijon mustard to a small bowl or jar. Add a pinch of salt and pepper to taste. Mix well and set aside.

Then, warm a small skillet over medium heat. Add the vegan butter and when it has melted, add the oats and almonds and season with the salt. Cook, stirring, for 5 minutes, or until the oats are golden brown.

Toss the romaine, spinach, berries and the vinaigrette together and top with the toasted almonds and oats mixture.

YIELD: 4 salads

NUTRITION INFORMATION PER SALAD
CALORIES: 269
FAT: 19 g
CARBS: 23 g
PROTEIN: 4 g

¼ cup (60 ml) extra virgin olive oil

2 tbsp (30 ml) white wine vinegar

1 tbsp (15 ml) maple syrup

1 tsp Dijon mustard

Pinch of salt and pepper

1 tbsp (14 g) vegan butter

½ cup (45 g) oats, gluten-free if needed

¼ cup (36 g) almonds

¼ tsp salt

2 cups (57 g) romaine lettuce

2 cups (60 g) spinach

2 cups (298 g) mixed berries

NUTRITION INFORMATION
PER SALAD
CALORIES: 325
FAT: 22 g
CARBS: 33 g
PROTEIN: 4 g

AGAVE LIME DRESSING

3 tbsp (45 ml) extra virgin olive oil

3 tbsp (45 ml) lime juice

1 tsp agave

Salt and pepper, to taste

TACO SALAD

½ tsp salt

1 tsp garlic powder

1 tsp dried oregano

1 tsp paprika

1 tsp chili powder

¼ tsp black pepper

½ tsp cumin

2 cups (268 g) diced sweet potatoes

1 tbsp (15 ml) extra virgin olive oil

4 cups (120 g) greens of choice,
I used romaine

1 cup (136 g) frozen, thawed corn, or
canned, rinsed and drained corn

1 cup (180 g) diced tomatoes

½ cup (80 g) finely chopped red or
green onion

1 cup (150 g) diced avocado

1 cup (240 ml) Corn and Black Bean
Salsa, optional (see page 116 or use
store-bought)

1 cup (63 g) tortilla chips, crushed

TACO SALAD IN A JAR

Next time you're in the mood for a healthy, filling salad when you're on the move, don't stop for takeout. Make this easy taco salad in a jar and walk out the door. This salad is delicious and really good for you! Filled with healthy vibrantly colored ingredients like sweet potatoes, corn, tomatoes and avocado, this tasty blend of vegetables will keep you feeling great when you're on the go.

To make the Agave Lime Dressing, in a small bowl whisk the olive oil, lime juice, agave, salt and pepper. Set aside.

To make the Taco Salad, in a small bowl, mix the salt, garlic powder, oregano, paprika, chili powder, black pepper and cumin. Set aside.

Preheat the oven to 400°F (205°C). Line a baking sheet with parchment paper.

Add the sweet potatoes to a medium-sized mixing bowl, drizzle with the olive oil, and season to taste with the spice mixture. Toss the potatoes to coat them well. Spread the sweet potatoes on the parchment-lined baking sheet and bake for 15 minutes. Remove the pan from the oven and use a spatula to flip the potatoes, then return them to the oven for another 10 to 15 minutes, until they are golden brown on the outside and tender on the inside. Allow them to cool before using in the salad.

Chop your greens of choice, then add 1 cup (30 g) of the greens to each of four jars, then top each with about one quarter of the corn, sweet potatoes, tomatoes, red onion, diced avocado, Corn and Black Bean Salsa, and top with crushed tortilla chips.

You can store the jars in the fridge for 2 to 3 days. Drizzle the Agave Lime Dressing into the jar before serving. Shake well to toss and then pour the contents of the jar into a bowl to serve.

CAESAR SALAD WITH CRISPY CHICKPEAS AND TEMPEH OR TOFU

Whenever my dad goes out to eat and there is a Caesar salad on the menu, he will order it. The man knows his Caesar salad so I needed to make sure to create a vegan version that would impress him. Traditional Caesar salad dressing has eggs and anchovies. But, this plant-based version gives you that creamy, tangy flavor without either. Add some additional protein by topping this salad with crispy chickpeas and tempeh or with pan-fried tofu! To save time, you can use ⅓ cup (33 g) of store-bought vegan Parmesan.

To make the Vegan Parmesan, add the roasted sunflower seeds, nutritional yeast, bread crumbs, garlic powder, onion powder, salt and olive oil to a blender. Blend until a crumble forms, then set aside.

To make the Marinated Tempeh & Crispy Chickpeas, in a mixing bowl, whisk the lemon juice, soy sauce, garlic powder and maple syrup. Chop the tempeh into 1-inch (2.5-cm) cubes, add it to the marinade and toss until evenly coated. Allow the tempeh to marinate for at least 10 minutes.

While the tempeh marinates, preheat the oven to 425°F (220°C) and line a baking sheet with aluminum foil. Drizzle the foil generously with olive oil and use a brush to evenly coat the foil. Alternatively, you can use olive oil, avocado oil or coconut oil spray to grease the foil.

Spread the marinated tempeh in a single layer on about two-thirds of the prepared baking sheet.

Fill the remainder of the baking sheet with the chickpeas. Season them with the garlic powder, paprika, salt and pepper. Drizzle with a little more olive oil and gently toss.

Bake the tempeh and chickpeas for 10 minutes, remove from the oven and flip the tempeh pieces and toss the chickpeas. Return the baking sheet to the oven and bake for another 5 to 10 minutes, or until the tempeh and chickpeas are golden brown.

(CONTINUED)

YIELD: 4 salads

NUTRITION INFORMATION FOR CHICKPEAS AND TEMPEH VARIATION, PER BOWL
CALORIES: 382
FAT: 18 g
CARBS: 37 g
PROTEIN: 23 g

NUTRITION INFORMATION FOR TOFU VARIATION (WITHOUT PARMESAN), PER BOWL
CALORIES: 400
FAT: 24 g
CARBS: 29 g
PROTEIN: 17 g

VEGAN PARMESAN
¼ cup (34 g) roasted sunflower seeds
2 tbsp (10 g) nutritional yeast
2 tbsp (14 g) vegan or gluten-free bread crumbs
½ tsp garlic powder
½ tsp onion powder
¼ tsp salt
½ tsp extra virgin olive oil

MARINATED TEMPEH & CRISPY CHICKPEAS
2 tbsp (30 ml) lemon juice
2 tbsp (30 ml) low-sodium soy sauce or coconut aminos
½ tsp garlic powder
1 tbsp (15 ml) maple syrup
1 (8-oz [226-g]) block of tempeh
Olive oil, for greasing
1 cup (164 g) canned chickpeas, rinsed and drained
½ tsp garlic powder
¼ tsp paprika
Salt and pepper

CRISPY TOFU

16 oz (454 g) extra-firm tofu, pressed (see Healthy Tip) and cut into 1-inch (2.5-cm) cubes

½ tsp garlic powder

¼ tsp salt

¼ tsp pepper

1 cup (240 ml) plain unsweetened almond milk

1 tsp cornstarch

½ cup (63 g) regular or gluten-free all-purpose flour

½ cup (54 g) vegan or gluten-free breadcrumbs

3 tbsp (45 ml) extra virgin olive oil

SALAD

4 cups (268 g) chopped kale

4 cups (170 g) chopped romaine

1 batch Vegan Caesar Dressing (page 101)

To make the Crispy Tofu, season the tofu cubes with the garlic powder, salt and pepper. In a medium bowl, whisk the almond milk and cornstarch. In a separate bowl, mix the flour and bread crumbs. Dip each piece of tofu in the almond milk mixture and then toss in the flour mixture.

Warm a skillet over medium heat. Add the olive oil and when it is warm, add the tofu to the skillet and cook for 3 to 5 minutes on each side, until both sides are golden. Remove the tofu from the skillet and place on a plate lined with a paper towel.

Assemble four bowls of salad with one quarter of the chopped kale and romaine, and either one quarter of the Crispy Tofu or one quarter of the Marinated Tempeh & Crispy Chickpeas, and as much Vegan Caesar Dressing and Vegan Parmesan cheese as you like.

HEALTHY TIP: To ensure that your tofu gets crispy, press it of excess water by either using a tofu press or paper towels. If using paper towels, simply slice the block of tofu into ½ inch (1.3 cm)-thick slices and then press them with paper towels until the majority of the water they were packaged in is absorbed.

ACKNOWLEDGMENTS

My third cookbook! Whoa!

When I wrote my first cookbook, *Easy Low-Cal Vegan Eats*, I had a dream of making this a three-book series. A cookbook, a baking book (*Light and Easy Vegan Baking*) and a breakfast and lunch book. A few years later, I am so excited to share the grand finale of my easy and low-calorie cookbook series. Don't worry, I'll be back with more books one day!

Over the years, I've learned so much, grown so much, and can honestly say that if it wasn't for God's hand in my life, and the support of my friends, my family and my super loyal audience, I wouldn't be here today. From the bottom of my heart, thank you all for believing in me, for trying my recipes and for allowing my food to become a small part of your lives. I hope my three cookbooks inspire healthy, balanced and delicious plant-based and gluten-free friendly dishes for years to come. And beautiful memories . . . because that's what it's all about.

To the incredible team at Page Street Publishing, a heartfelt thank you for seeing my vision and working with me to make it happen.

To my parents, siblings and friends, who constantly encourage me in chasing my dreams, who never seem to mind being my in-house photographers and videographers, and who are always on standby to be my recipe tasters: My heart is full because of you and these three books wouldn't have been possible without you.

To my readers, you guys have been with me since day one. You've given me feedback, you've encouraged me and you've inspired me to keep going, to keep creating and to keep sharing my love through food. I cannot thank you enough for trusting me to create vegan and gluten-free recipes for you and the ones you love. This book is truly for you.

ABOUT THE AUTHOR

JILLIAN GLENN, author of the best-selling *Easy Low-Cal Vegan Eats* and *Light and Easy Vegan Baking* cookbooks is a popular vegan and gluten-free friendly recipe creator, blogger and a trusted source for easy low-calorie vegan recipes. Her well-known blog, Peanut Butter and Jilly, reaches hundreds of thousands each year and has become a favored guide for better-for-you vegan eats and sweets.

Jillian has received national press from NBC, CBS, ABC's *Good Morning America* and more. All of her recipes are plant-based, almost all of them can be made gluten-free and they are absolutely mouthwatering. Jillian prides herself on always using affordable, easy-to-find ingredients and simple instructions to create her crave-worthy comfort foods. She has a certification in nutrition, prioritizes health and wellness and also believes in balance. Because of this she never deprives her sweet tooth and thanks to her easy recipes, you won't have to either.

To learn more and connect with Jillian, check out her blog, PeanutButterandJilly.com

INDEX